INTERMEDIATE
EXERCISES IN ENGLISH

INTERMEDIATE
EXERCISES IN ENGLISH

BY

E. E. REYNOLDS

**Author of *Exercises in English*, etc.
Editor of Marlowe's
Edward II, etc.**

CAMBRIDGE

AT THE UNIVERSITY PRESS

1931

CAMBRIDGE
UNIVERSITY PRESS

University Printing House, Cambridge CB2 8BS, United Kingdom

Cambridge University Press is part of the University of Cambridge.

It furthers the University's mission by disseminating knowledge in the pursuit of education, learning and research at the highest international levels of excellence.

www.cambridge.org
Information on this title: www.cambridge.org/9781316612583

© Cambridge University Press 1931

First published 1931
First paperback edition 2016

A catalogue record for this publication is available from the British Library

ISBN 978-1-316-61258-3 Paperback

CONTENTS

PREFACE

The present collection of exercises is intended for use during the second and third years of a School Certificate Course in English. The work covered leads up to my *Exercises in English*, and the two books together will supply a sufficient range of practice for all but the early stages of the normal syllabus.

No explanatory matter is included, partly to economise space so that a considerable bulk of material for practice could be included, and partly because explanation is best given by word of mouth by the teacher, and not read from a book by the pupil.

§ I. *Grammar*. The majority of the sentences in this section have been drawn from books so that the pupil is dealing with the language in its normal expression, and not as it can be used for illustrating particular grammatical points. Sentences in other languages should also be used for analysis to emphasise the fact that Grammar is not peculiar to English, but equally concerns Latin, French, and other languages. Oral work will be found most productive at this stage.

§ II. *Spelling and Punctuation*. It is important that stress should be laid on accuracy in spelling and punctuation; it is however better for the pupil to keep lists of his own errors, rather than to do too many formal exercises. Exercise VIII generally captures interest—not an easy achievement in such a mechanical subject.

§ III. *Vocabulary*. In order to enlarge the vocabulary and also to encourage the use of a Dictionary as much as possible, many words are used in this section that would not normally be part of the pupil's knowledge. The passages in Exercise XXVI have been taken from the popular stories that appeal to boys and girls of 13 and 14. The teacher of English should be acquainted with this type of writing, as it provides a useful guide to the pupils' range of vocabulary.

§ IV. *Note-making and Précis*. Definite instruction and practice should be given in note-making. To be able to make well-organised and succinct notes is of considerable value, and the pupil should acquire this skill as soon as possible in his career. The passages given offer a wide range of types, but further practice should be chosen from the school text-books, and from newspapers.

§ V. *Paraphrase*. The passages in Exercise I have been arranged in chronological order (1470–1707) so that they can also be used for illustrating the major characteristics in the development of English prose style. The verse extracts in Exercise II have been chosen for their content rather than for their form, but they will be found useful as additional examples of prosody.

§ VI. *Study of Prose Passages*. Close study of selected short passages of prose is a valuable aid to the writing of English, and to an appreciation of style and method of presentation. The questions set on each extract direct the pupil's attention to matters of vocabulary and expression. A number of topics for writing are also given, not for the purpose of encouraging the imitation of the originals; the passages are useful points of departure for exercising the imagination, and for suggesting points of view. Similar exercises should be set on other passages chosen from the books read in school.

§ VII. *Composition.* This section contains nearly 400 subjects for writing; the requirements vary from a short answer to a more elaborate essay. The work will gain in value if subjects are discussed in class before the writing is attempted. It is hoped that each pupil will find a number of his own interests in the wide variety of topics suggested.

§ VIII. *Verse.* A few simple exercises in verse forms are given. These should not be used too frequently, as they are but minor aids to the enjoyment of poetry.

E. E. R.

February 1931

I. Simple sentences for revision work:

    i. Two days afterwards they bathed again.

    ii. Bevis shaved the fir-pole for the mast.

    iii. They played round the huge sycamore trunks above the quarry.

    iv. Mark hurled the bar to the other end of the cellar.

    v. He hit the lock a tremendous bang.

    vi. Presently he came quietly back from a gap by a hollow willow.

    vii. They cleared away the loose sand and earth at the foot of the cliff.

    viii. A piece of tar-cord was inserted in a long stick split at the end.

    ix. Isn't it jolly to be seven thousand miles from anywhere?

    x. There are strange sounds here at night.

    xi. "Go on, Pan!"
       "Catch him!"
       "Fetch him!"
       "He's got him!"
       "He's in the weeds!"
       "He can't get back. The duck drags in the weeds."
       "Pan! Pan! Here!"
       "He can't do it!"
       "He's caught."
       "Not he."

    xii. Then he lay down with a contented grunt at the master's feet.

    xiii. He pointed out the spoors going to and from the drinking-place.

xiv. I used to take Jock with me everywhere.

xv. They learned to give him a very wide berth.

xvi. It is easy enough to lose oneself in the Bush-veld.

xvii. Five of the puppies were fat strong yellow little chaps with dark muzzles.

xviii. For several days he took no further notice of me.

xix. You must not feed another man's dog.

xx. He again very slowly and carefully began to step forward.

xxi. He must find meat.

xxii. Now the grey cub had lived all his days on a level floor.

xxiii. There was something calling to him out there in the open.

xxiv. In the third year of his life there came a great famine to the Mackenzie Indians.

xxv. A heavy price of gold was upon his head.

xxvi. Sir John began life as a bricklayer.

xxvii. Victoria Station is every morning the scene of romance.

xxviii. Fabulous millions are locked away underground in the safe deposits of London.

xxix. Work is started fairly early in the morning.

xxx. The Chairman uttered a few words of welcome.

xxxi. This manner of conducting business amazed me.

xxxii. In 855 the Viking host wintered in Sheppey.

xxxiii. The tortoise does not grumble at the English winter; it evades it by the simple process of self-burial.

II. Pick out the adjective clauses:

i. There was not a beggar upon the country-side who did not know him.

ii. My story is one which you may well treasure up in your minds.

iii. His voice was the most tremendous that I have ever listened to.

iv. My father, who was as active as he was strong, sprang aside.

v. There were other shows which I might see for nothing.

vi. A constant feud prevailed between the scholars who attended the day-school and the lads who studied under our master.

vii. His son William is still carrying on the business which is larger and more prosperous than of old.

viii. We both broke into a roar of laughter which lasted for some time.

ix. I have a mission here which cannot be neglected.

x. It is two-thirds full of gold which the worthy gentleman is hoarding.

xi. In my hands is the proclamation which our royal leader hath sent in advance of him.

xii. The interior, which consisted of a single great hall, the empty warehouse in which wool used to be stored, was all alight with lamps and candles.

xiii. These cliffs run out into the sea, and numerous little harbours and bays are formed in their broken surface, which are dry half the day, but can float a good-sized boat at half-tide.

xiv. The road along which I had travelled was a lonely one.

xv. He had a fine high forehead from which his hair was brushed straight back.

III. Pick out the adverb clauses:

i. Before the robbers were able to reach these chambers, they had many difficulties to surmount and problems to solve.

ii. They had done so much themselves that there seemed little more for him to do.

iii. Richer treasures still may await the spade of the excavator, for the deserts hide the relics of many nations.

iv. As I neared the spring on my homeward road, I saw him standing beside the track.

v. The Chairman now invited us to interrogate the candidates, if we wished.

vi. Although the force of circumstances has brought me thus low, I am by birth and education a gentleman.

vii. If I choose, I can march you off to jail for a common housebreaker.

viii. This did not affect him a jot, since he held precisely the same opinion of his neighbours.

ix. The moon, when I fell asleep, had not surmounted the ridge.

x. As he spoke he drew a flat box from his pocket.

xi. You must follow this sheep-track until you come on another and broader pathway.

xii. Let us ride past it, for it is little out of our way.

xiii. The movement was so sudden and so unexpected that there was a dead silence for a few seconds.

xiv. If these men are so close we have no great time for preparation.

xv. Whilst this conversation had been proceeding, we had been walking our horses down the winding track.

IV. Pick out the noun clauses:

i. He told his son that he proposed setting out for London immediately.

ii. It became known in the land that I had money.

iii. Even allowing for the lapse of months and years, Mabruk could not believe that he would ever grow content with that life of herded sheep.

iv. What I most admire is his calmness.

v. Allah knows I have not wronged him in the least.

vi. The native carriers declared that they would go to the River Lomame, but no farther.

vii. We hoped that by some miracle he might have escaped.

viii. I noticed that the upper parts of the walls were of sun-dried brick.

ix. Every moment I expected that we should be hurled down the chasm.

x. I fancied that everything was enchanted.

xi. I will very soon let you know how little I think of you and all your barbarous Franks.

xii. It was clear that he had no intention of carrying out his promise.

xiii. Once more I realised that Cyprus was a land of many climates.

xiv. It is noticeable that black pelts become common among animals in domestication.

xv. A suggestion that they were typically English would be received by them as an insult.

xvi. It is true that a crocodile farm is not so simple as a poultry farm.

xvii. It is obvious that stars have a fascination for some people.

V. Complex and compound sentences for analysis:

i. It is impossible to walk about London without being struck by the number of people who seem to have time on their hands.

ii. An English village awakens slowly, as men awaken who are not harshly stirred.

iii. Many favourite plants attract superstitions, and the daring belief survives in country villages that a primrose plant buried head downwards will send up blossoms of the shade of dull purple familiar in old gardens.

iv. It is in June that lawns come into their own.

v. Few things are more restful at the beginning of a holiday than a long journey in a swift train, during which the traveller, in his corner seat facing the engine, watches the country unroll itself.

vi. Some people like to eat to music, which saves them the mental effort of talking.

vii. It must be admitted that gardeners as a race have a very poor notion of making a bonfire.

viii. In a book published not long ago there appeared a picture entitled "The Author and his Best Friend", the friend being a remarkably capacious waste-paper basket.

ix. It needs courage to career about the streets of London, even at night, in running shorts.

x. The Persians and the Chinese can do anything with colours, because they know how to proportion them.

xi. I came to the house of a rich man, and as I saw him standing in the light of a front window I called out to him from a distance.

xii. In the dusk he could not make out who I was, but judging by my voice he took me for an educated man, one of his own class.

xiii. I had taken my ticket a fortnight only in advance, just in time to secure the last berth in the sleeping-car which runs to Brindisi every Friday from Calais.

xiv. I examined the aperture in the bank of rock, and I found that a stone staircase led down to a series of vaulted rooms.

xv. He answered that the river below us was rarely anything more than a dry bed of pebbles, just as it was now.

xvi. We lay in the tent and listened to the wind with the luxurious feeling that comes of good shelter.

xvii. When he had finished his shaving operations, he looked round the scantily appointed dressing-table for something upon which to wipe his razor.

xviii. In another moment the occupant of the cottage had lit the lamp that stood ready on the table, and had turned towards the two men.

xix. As he picked up the lantern afterwards he saw that his hands were smeared with his blood.

xx. There are islands in the Pacific where one of your prime aims in life is not to be killed in your bed the next time your house is blown down by a hurricane.

xxi. For a little while the keen eyes of the lad sought for handholds and footholds; then he squeezed himself into a crevice at the side of the big rock and began to worm his way upward.

xxii. When we first started the work of drawing out the plan and elevations, we were puzzled to find that the different measurements never seemed to agree.

xxiii. Do you realise that we have only a few days left of our holiday?

xxiv. He had no dignity and no system in his conduct of a class, but would often go to sleep, with a handkerchief over his face, his chair tilted back, and his feet on his writing-desk.

xxv. "What would happen", I asked once, "if anyone went into that wood?"

xxvi. If you try to cut a hole through thick ice with an ordinary axe it will not be long before you hit the top edges with your fingers.

xxvii. Whoever does this will have great joy and happiness, but to those who neglect this will come misfortune.

xxviii. Although the expert knowledge of the legionaries was required for the construction of the wall, they did not form the garrison which defended it.

xxix. If the inhabitant of equatorial Africa is adapted to a hot climate to some extent, he nevertheless suffers and finds it difficult to maintain regular hard work over long periods.

xxx. It is clear that water can only flow through a permeable rock if there is a means of exit at a lower level.

xxxi. Do what you will: but while you stay with me, I follow this river until I come to the point where it is known.

xxxii. Why should anyone want to kill Davies, and why should Davies, the soul of modesty and simplicity, imagine that anyone wanted to kill him?

xxxiii. That two days later I should be found pacing the deck of the Flushing steamer with a ticket for Hamburg in my pocket may seem a strange thing.

VI. Frame sentences to satisfy the following schemes:

i. Main clause—noun clause (object).

ii. Main clause—adjective clause.

iii. Main clause—adverb clause (manner).

iv. Main clause—adverb clause (manner)—adverb clause (condition).

v. Main clause—noun clause (object)—adjective clause.

vi. Adverb clause (reason)—adjectival clause—noun clause (object)—main clause.

vii. Main clause—noun clause (object)—adverb clause (time).

viii. Two co-ordinate main clauses—adjectival clause.

ix. Adverbial clause (time)—main clause—adjectival clause.

x. Main clause—adjective clause—adverb clause.

xi. Adverb clause (time)—main clause—adverb clause (place).

xii. Main clause—adverb clause (purpose).

xiii. Two co-ordinate main clauses—noun clause (object)
—adjective clause.

xiv. Two adjective clauses—main clause—adverb clause
(reason).

xv. Main clause—noun clause (apposition)—adverb
clause (purpose).

VII. State the person, number, tense and mood of each
verb in these sentences:

  i. The party did not realise what it was up against.

  ii. Of course everyone knows it by heart.

  iii. If you fasten a hat-peg on a door, you must fasten it
with the slope upwards, otherwise the hat will slip off.

  iv. He would hardly have forfeited his position if he had
deserved to retain it.

  v. Don't brawl here!

  vi. The best way will be to put it to the vote, and then
everybody will be satisfied.

  vii. You must not sit together.

viii. Madame, as we cannot fly, would it not be well to
receive the troops as if we did not know they were
coming?

  ix. The coach is to be got ready, and my lady will ride
away at once.

  x. I am a stranger, sir, but, as for being poor, I think
I need not be charged with poverty, till I seek money
of somebody.

VIII. What is the function of a preposition? What other
parts of speech may be used as prepositions? Give
examples.

IX. Pick out the joining words in the following sentences, and state what part of speech each is:

   i. The climbing was difficult, but that was expected.

  ii. It was by that time one o'clock, and by six it would be dark.

 iii. The more prudent preferred undertakings which they could see.

 iv. Things were going so well with him that he had no mind to spare for trifles, and no time to look aside.

  v. Others sneaked off to the churchyard, or to some neighbouring nook, and there opened the journal with trembling fingers.

 vi. He told himself and strove to believe that he could deal with it when it pleased him.

vii. Clerks rushing into the court, hatless and demented, plunged into clerks rushing out equally demented, yet flew on their course without look or word, as if unconscious of the impact.

X. The sentences given in the preceding exercises of this section can also be used for the following questions:

   i. Compare the adjectives and adverbs.

  ii. Give the past participle of each verb.

 iii. Pick out the auxiliary verbs.

 iv. Which of the nouns and pronouns have case inflection? State the case of each.

  v. Pick out adjective phrases and substitute where possible a single word for each.

 vi. Pick out the adverbs and where possible substitute an adverb phrase for each.

vii. Pick out the objects of the prepositions.

XI. Explain, with examples, the differences between a sentence, a phrase and a clause.

XII. How would you determine whether a word is used as a preposition or an adverb?

XIII. What is a dependent clause? Give examples of the different kinds.

XIV. Explain, with examples, the different uses of *shall* and *will*.

XV. Explain, with examples, the use of the following terms in grammar:

limitation, modify, attributive, comparison, complement, relative, distributive, reflexive, collective, auxiliary.

XVI. Write sentences containing the plural forms of the following nouns:

fly, monkey, hero, wharf, cargo, terminus, governor-general, fish, innings, corps, Lord Justice, porridge, penny, chief, latchkey, foot-rule, portmanteau, torch, cuckoo, goose.

XVII. State the case of each noun and pronoun in the following sentences:

i. On the soft ground amid the tree-trunks lay a helmet.

ii. The great Roman road from Lincoln to Cirencester, known as the Fosse Way, crosses the valley of the Coln some seven miles short of the latter town.

iii. I don't know that I need it.

iv. The fact that you had to do your utmost is enough.

v. As soon as ever I was strong enough, I started.

vi. I don't know if this satisfied my father: but I know that he meant it to satisfy me.

vii. A puff of north-east wind shot over the hill.

viii. As I climbed the stairs he came in from the porch and met me on the landing.

ix. Something must be done.

x. He pointed to a statue of Saint Anne which adorned a porch of the Church of the Madeleine.

XVIII. State the kind of each noun and pronoun in the above sentences.

XIX. State the antecedent word of each relative pronoun in these sentences:

i. He was attracted by the light which he saw.

ii. The miller stood motionless, leaning on the fowling-piece which he carried.

iii. Nature had given him qualities with a temperament which forbade him to make use of them.

iv. He returned to the table which he had quitted.

v. "Who was that?" he asked.

vi. Opposite to him was the man whom he had last seen in Paris.

vii. Outside Louis, who loved all horses, stood with her bridle over his arm and talked to the Englishman's horse.

viii. Here they did find a sort of ostler, to whom the horse could be committed.

ix. May I, without indiscretion, know whom I have the privilege of addressing?

x. The hayloft in which I stood ran the whole length of the outbuildings, the ground floor of which consisted of storeroom, byre, and what was once a stable.

XX. Pick out the verbs in the sentences in Exercises XVII and XIX; state whether each is used transitively or intransitively.

XXI. Re-write in the passive voice where possible:

i. The French had explored the Great Lakes, and had crossed the maze of waterways beyond Lake Superior.

ii. He selected a point on the south shore, and there constructed Fort Chipewyan.

iii. For food they carried some bags of pemmican and some corn; these, however, they used as emergency rations, and they relied normally on the fish and game which they secured on the way.

iv. They had still to endure the hardest part of the journey.

v. He had discovered one of the greatest rivers of the world.

vi. Volleys of musketry greeted the new year.

vii. On the 21st they cached a bag of pemmican in a hole, and lighted a fire to hide all traces of the excavation.

viii. His interpreter assured the Indians on the other bank of his friendliness.

ix. They met the Coast Indians six days' journey along this trail, and exchanged their own furs and leather for short iron bars, brass, copper, and beads, all of which they procured from white men who came in ships.

x. They were generally able to procure a few fish from the natives.

XXII. Re-write in the active voice:

i. They were surrounded by snowy mountains.

ii. Gradually the women were calmed and won over by presents.

iii. They were regaled with a plentiful meal of salmon, prepared in a number of ways.

    iv. He was received without surprise, and was conducted to the largest house in the village.

    v. They were alarmed to see men fetching their weapons.

    vi. Two trading posts should be built by the government.

   vii. He was elected in 1795 to the Beaver Club.

  viii. The two companies were to be united and the name of the Hudson's Bay Company was to be retained.

    ix. The voyageurs were employed in transport, in fishing, and in other duties about the trading posts.

    x. Delayed on the way up, his canoes were checked by ice before reaching Portage La Loche.

XXIII. Name the *-ing* forms in these sentences, and give reasons for your decisions:

    i. In the Alps the actual climbing is just as hard as any in the Himalayas.

    ii. Concurrently with collecting the money, the Committee concerned itself with collecting the men and purchasing the equipment and stores.

   iii. When the Committee had decided upon selecting him he was asked to come and see the Chairman.

    iv. The letters brought out in glaring relief the value of training and experience.

    v. You cannot imagine how living things can subsist there.

    vi. When the men were objecting to carrying loads, he shamed them into doing it by strapping one on his own back and carrying it a whole stage.

   vii. It could be argued of course that inhaling oxygen was no more unsporting than taking a cup of beef-tea.

  viii. Getting into frozen boots and making something hot for breakfast occupied time.

    ix. A dead numbing feeling was creeping up their limbs.

    x. By effecting the rescue they had reaffirmed that principle of loyal comradeship upon which all mountaineering must be based.

XXIV. Pick out from the last three exercises all the adjectives and adverbs and classify them.

XXV. What are the functions of the infinitive forms in the following sentences?

   i. He decided to send him for a cruise on board a merchant vessel.

  ii. It was not easy to obtain the necessary information.

 iii. To know the extent of that lake would be worth some trouble.

  iv. His business was to make a treaty there.

   v. To show fear by going another way would have been fatal.

  vi. He became too ill even to be carried.

 vii. The natives clearly wanted to express themselves.

viii. To make good this statement it is only necessary to give a bare outline of the facts.

  ix. A halt was made to replenish the water supply.

   x. He was lodged in an outhouse the better to deceive the servants.

XXVI. State the part of speech of each italicised word in the following sentences:

   i. They came one *after* the other. He grumbled *after* the match was over. Jill came tumbling *after*. *After* he had left, there was a sense of relief.

  ii. There were many other reasons *besides*. There were many other reasons *besides* that one. You will find that a nuisance, *besides* you don't really need it.

 iii. He had to appear *before* the judge. *Before* he went on his holidays he insured his baggage. He had never done such a thing *before*. I would rather die, *before* doing such a thing.

  iv. I will come *as* soon *as* I can. He looks *as* if he had seen a ghost. We lost the train *as* he was late in getting up. I had exactly the same trouble *as* you. Do *as* you like.

XXVII. Re-write the following passages changing the direct into indirect (reported), and the indirect (reported) into direct speech wherever possible:

(a)   *Enter* SIR WILLIAM HONEYWOOD and JARVIS

Sir Will. Good Jarvis, make no apologies for this honest bluntness. Fidelity, like yours, is the best excuse for every freedom.

Jarvis. I can't help being blunt, and being very angry too, when I hear you talk of disinheriting so good, so worthy a young gentleman as your nephew, my master. All the world loves him.

Sir Will. Say rather, that he loves all the world; that is his fault.

Jarvis. I'm sure there is no part of it more dear to him than you are, though he has not seen you since he was a child.

Sir Will. What signifies his affection to me, or how can I be proud of a place in a heart where every sharper and coxcomb find an easy entrance?

Jarvis. I grant you that he's rather too good-natured; that he's too much every man's man; that he laughs this minute with one, and cries the next with another; but whose instructions may he thank for all this?

Sir Will. Not mine, sure? My letters to him during my employment in Italy, taught him only that philosophy which might prevent, not defend his errors.

OLIVER GOLDSMITH, *The Good-Natur'd Man*

(b)   *Pasha.* The Englishman is welcome; most blessed among hours is this, the hour of his coming.

Dragoman (to the traveller). The Pasha pays you his compliments.

Traveller. Give him my best compliments in return and say I'm delighted to have the honour of seeing him.

Dragoman (to the Pasha). His lordship, this Englishman, Lord of London, Scorner of Ireland, Suppressor of France, has quitted his governments, and left his enemies to breathe for a moment, and has crossed the broad waters in strict disguise, with a small but eternally faithful retinue of followers, in order that he might look upon the bright countenance of the Pasha among Pashas—the Pasha of the everlasting Pashalik of Karagholookoldour.

Traveller (to his dragoman). What on earth have you been saying about London? The Pasha will be taking me for a mere cockney. Have not I told you *always* to say that I am from a branch of the family of Mudcombe Park, and that I am to be a magistrate for the county of Bedfordshire, only I've not qualified, and that I should have been a deputy-lieutenant if it had not been for the extraordinary conduct of Lord Mountpromise, and that I was a candidate for Goldborough at the last election, and that I should have won easy if my committee had not been bought. I wish to Heaven that if you *do* say anything about me, you'd tell the simple truth.

A. W. KINGLAKE, Eothen

(*c*) Little more worth remembering occurred during the play, at the end of which Jones asked him, "Which of the players he had liked best?" To this he answered, with some appearance of indignation at the question, "The king, without doubt". "Indeed, Mr Partridge," says Mrs Miller, "you are not of the same opinion with the town; for they are all agreed, that Hamlet is acted by the best player who ever was on the stage." "He the best player!" cries Partridge, with a contemptuous sneer, "why, I could act as well as he myself. I am sure, if I had seen a ghost, I should have looked in the very same manner, and done just as he did. And then, to be sure, in that scene, as you called it, between him and his mother, where you told me he acted so fine, why, Lord help me, any man, that is, any good man, that had such a mother, would have done exactly the same. I know you are only joking with me; but indeed, madam, though I was never at a play in London, yet I have seen acting before in the country; and the king for my money; he speaks all his words distinctly, half as loud again as the other.—Anybody may see he is an actor."

While Mrs Miller was thus engaged in conversation with Partridge, a lady came up to Mr Jones, whom he immediately knew to be Mrs Fitzpatrick. She said, she had seen him from the other part of the gallery, and had taken that opportunity of speaking to him, as she had something to say, which might be of great service to himself.

HENRY FIELDING, Tom Jones

(*d*) William was so uneasy at losing this opportunity, that he pressed us earnestly to go up to Japan to find out these men. He told us that if it was nothing but to recover thirteen honest

poor men from a kind of captivity, which they would otherwise never be redeemed from, and where, perhaps, they might,
some time or other, be murdered by the barbarous people, in
defence of their idolatry, it were very well worth our while,
and it would be, in some measure, making amends for the
mischiefs we had done in the world; but we, that had no
concern upon us for the mischiefs we had done, had much less
about any satisfactions to be made for it, so he found that kind
of discourse would weigh very little with us. Then he pressed
us very earnestly to let him have the sloop to go by himself, and
I told him I would not oppose it; but when he came to the
sloop none of the men would go with him; for the case was
plain, they had all a share in the cargo of the great ship, as well
as in that of the sloop, and the richness of the cargo was such
that they would not leave it by any means; so poor William,
much to his mortification, was obliged to give it over. What
became of those thirteen men, or whether they are not there
still, I can give no account of.

DANIEL DEFOE, *Captain Singleton*

(e) He had heard of ships, too, beating up the Gulf of
Finland against a head wind, and having a ship heave in sight
astern, overhaul, and pass them, with as fair a wind as could
blow and all studding-sails out, and find she was from Finland.

"Oh, oh," said he; "I've seen too much of them men to
want to see 'em 'board a ship."

As I still doubted, he said he would leave it to John, who
was the oldest seaman aboard, and would know if anybody did.
John, to be sure, was the oldest, and at the same time the most
ignorant man in the ship; but I consented to have him called.
The cook stated the matter to him, and John, as I anticipated,
sided with the cook, and said that he himself had been in a ship
where they had a head wind for a fortnight, and the captain
found out at last that one of the men, whom he had had some
hard words with a short time before, was a Finn, and immediately told him if he didn't stop the head wind he would shut
him down in the fore-peak. The Finn would not give in, and
the captain shut him down in the fore-peak, and would not give
him anything to eat. The Finn held out for a day and a half,
when he could not stand it any longer, and did something or
other which brought the wind round again, and they let him
up.

"There," said the cook, "what do you think o' dat?"

I told him I had no doubt it was true, and that it would have been odd if the wind had not changed in fifteen days, Finn or no Finn.

R. H. DANA, *Two Years Before the Mast*

(*f*) "Robin, I believe," said young Gamwell carelessly; "I think they call him Robin."

"Is that all you know of him?" said Sir Ralph.

"What more should I know of him?" said young Gamwell.

"Then I can tell you," said Sir Ralph, "he is the outlawed Earl of Huntingdon, on whose head is set so large a price."

"Ay, is he?" said young Gamwell, in the same careless manner.

"He is a prize worth the taking", said Sir Ralph.

"No doubt", said young Gamwell.

"How think you?" said Sir Ralph: "are the foresters his adherents?"

"I cannot say", said young Gamwell.

"Is your peasantry loyal and well-disposed?" said Sir Ralph.

"Passing loyal", said young Gamwell.

"If I should call on them in the king's name", said Sir Ralph, "think you they would aid and assist?"

"Most likely they would," said young Gamwell, "one side or the other."

"Ay, but which side?" said the knight.

"That remains to be tried", said young Gamwell.

"I have King Henry's commission", said the knight, "to apprehend this earl that was. How would you advise me to act, being, as you see, without attendant force?"

"I would advise you", said young Gamwell, "to take yourself off without delay, unless you would relish the taste of a volley of arrows, a shower of stones, and a hailstorm of cudgel-blows, which would not be turned aside by a God save King Henry."

T. L. PEACOCK, *Maid Marian*

(*g*) Mr Pickwick observed that fame was dear to the heart of every man. Poetic fame was dear to the heart of his friend Snodgrass; the fame of conquest was equally dear to his friend Tupman; and the desire of earning fame in the sports of the field, the air, and the water, was uppermost in the breast of his friend Winkle. He (Mr Pickwick) would not deny that he was influenced by human passions, and human feelings—(cheers)—possibly by human weaknesses—(loud cries of "No"); but this he would say, that if ever the fire of self-importance broke out in his bosom, the desire to benefit the human race in preference effectually quenched it. The praise of mankind was his Swing; philanthropy was his insurance office. (Vehement cheering.) He had felt some pride—he acknowledged it freely, and let his enemies make the most of it—he had felt some pride when he presented his Tittlebatian Theory to the world; it might be celebrated or it might not. (A cry of "It is", and great cheering.) He would take the assertion of that honourable Pickwickian whose voice he had just heard—it was celebrated; but if the fame of that treatise were to extend to the farthest confines of the known world, the pride with which he should reflect on the authorship of that production would be as nothing compared with the pride with which he looked around him on this, the proudest moment of his existence. (Cheers.) He was a humble individual. (No, no.) Still he could not but feel that they had selected him for a service of great honour, and of some danger. Travelling was in a troubled state, and the minds of coachmen were unsettled. Let them look abroad and contemplate the scenes which were enacting around them. Stage coaches were upsetting in all directions, horses were bolting, boats were overturning, and boilers were bursting. (Cheers—a voice, "No".) No! (Cheers.) Let that honourable Pickwickian who cried "No" so loudly come forward and deny it, if he could. (Cheers.) Who was it that cried "No"? (Enthusiastic cheering.) Was it some vain and disappointed man—he would not say haberdasher—(loud cheers)—who, jealous of the praise which had been—perhaps undeservedly—bestowed on his (Mr Pickwick's) researches, and smarting under the censure which had been heaped upon his own feeble attempts at rivalry, now took this vile and calumnious mode of——

Mr BLOTTON (of Aldgate) rose to order. Did the honourable Pickwickian allude to him? (Cries of "Order", "Chair", "Yes", "No", "Go on", "Leave off", etc.)

Mr PICKWICK would not put up to be put down by clamour. He *had* alluded to the honourable gentleman. (Great excitement.)

C. DICKENS, The Pickwick Papers

I. Complete the following words by inserting *ie* or *ei*:

p rce, rec ve, s ze, p ce, bel ve, s ge, conc t, c ling, f ld, br f, n ce, dec t, v w, n ther, rev w, rec pt, f rce.

II. Give the plural of:

loaf, knife, chief, mischief, wharf, staff, lady, cliff, army, cargo.

III. Give the possessive form of each of the following words in the plural and singular:

ox, lady, boy, watch, child, women, hero, church, fairy, Jones, James.

IV. Complete the following words with *-ance* or *-ence*:

deliver-, pres-, impati-, temper-, rever-, guid-, ignor-, allow-, dist-, abund-, correspond-.

V. Complete the following by adding *-able* or *-ible*:

remark-, respons-, forc-, tract-, unalter-, laugh-, read-, sens-, resist-, poss-, vis-, ami-.

VI. Write sentences to bring out the differences in meaning between the words in each of these groups:

piece, peace; fair, fare; sail, sale; week, weak; wrap, rap; coarse, course; guilt, gilt; principal, principle.

VII. Complete the following agent words by adding *-er* or *-or*:

preach-, auth-, murder-, emper-, tail-, prison-, butch-, sail-, conjur-, act-.

VIII. Re-write the following passages with modernised spelling and punctuation; don't change anything else:

(a)   Twyse Robyn shot aboute,
    And ever he cleved the wande
And so dyde good Gylberte,
    With the whyte hand;

Lytell Johan and good Scathelocke,
    For nothyng wolde they spare;
When they fayled of the garlonde,
    Robyn smote them full sair.

At the last shot that Robyn shot,
    For all his frendes fare
Yet he fayled of the garlonde,
    Thre fyngers and mair.

(Ballad)

(b) Huntyng of the hare with grehoundes is a righte good solace for men that be studiouse; or them to whom nature hath nat gyven personage or courage apte for the warres. And also for gentilwomen, which fere neither sonne nor wynde for appairing their beautie. And peraventure they shall be thereat lasse idell than they shulde be at home in their chambres.

Kylling of dere with bowes or grehundes serveth well for the potte (as is the commune saynge) and therefore it muste of necessitie be sometyme used. But it contayneth therein no commendable solace or exercise in comparison to the other fourme of hunting, if it be diligently perceived.

As for haukyng, I can finde no notable remembrance that it was used of auncient tyme amonge noble princes.

Sir Thomas Elyot, *The Governor*

(c) Howe moche profited the feate in swymmynge to the valiant Julius Cesar! who at the bataile of Alexandri, on a bridge beinge abandoned of his people for the multitude of his enemyes, whiche oppressed them, whan he moughte no lenger sustaine the shotte of dartes and arowes, he boldly lepte into the see, and swamme the space of CC pasis to one of his shyppes, drawynge his cote-armure with his teethe after hym, that his enemies shulde nat attayne it. And also that it moughte somewhat defende hym from theyr arowes. And that more mervaile was, holdynge in his hande above the water certayne lettres, whiche a litle before he had receyved from the Senate.

SIR THOMAS ELYOT, The Governor

(*d*) Yet all *swimming* must needes be ill for the head, considering the continuall exhalation, which ascendeth still from the water into the head. *Swimming* in hot waters softeneth that which is hardened, warmeth that which is cooled, nimbleth the jointes which are benumbed, thinneth the skinne, which is thickened, and yet it troubleth the head, weakneth the bodie, disperTheth humours, but dissilveth them not. *Swimming* in cold water doth strengthen the naturall heat, bycause it beates it in: it maketh verie good and quick digestion: it breaketh superfluous humours, it warmeth the inward partes, yet long tarying in it hurts the sinews, and takes awaye the hearing. Thus much concerning *swimming*, which can neither do children harme in learning, if the maister be wise, nor the common weale but good, being once learned, if either private daunger or publike attempt do bid them adventure. For he that oweth a life to his countrey, if he die on lande, he doeth his duetie, and if drowne in water, his duetie is not drowned.

RICHARD MULCASTER, Positions

(*e*) During the tyme that the famous Citie of Constantinople remained in the handes of the Christians, emongst many other noble menne, that kepte their abidyng in that florishing citie, there was one whose name was Apolonius, a worthie duke, who beyng but a verie yong man, and euen then newe come to his possessions whiche were verie greate, leuied a mightie bande of menne, at his owne proper charges, with whom he serued against the Turke, duryng the space of one whole yere, in whiche tyme although it were very shorte, this yong duke so behaued hym selfe, as well by prowesse and valiaunce shewed with his owne handes, as otherwise, by his wisedome and liberalitie, vsed towardes his souldiors, that all the worlde was filled with the fame of this noble duke. When he had thus spent one yeares seruice, he caused his trompet to sounde a retraite, and gatheryng his companie together, and imbarkyng theim selues he sette saile, holdying his course towardes Constantinople: but beeyng vppon the sea, by the extremitie of a tempest whiche sodainly fell, his fleete was deseuered some one way, and some an other, but he hym selfe recouered the Ile of Cypres, where he was worthily receiued by Pontus duke and gouernour of the same ile, with whom he lodged, while his shippes were newe repairyng.

This Pontus that was lorde and gouernour of this famous ile, was an auncient duke, and had two children, a sonne and a daughter, his sonne was named Siluio, of whom hereafter we shall haue further occasion to speake, but at this instant he was in the partes of Africa, seruyng in the warres.

BARNABY RICH, *Apolonius and Silla*

(*f*) Therfore sayd Arthur vnto Syr Bedwere, "Take thou Excalybur my good swerde and goo with it to yonder water syde & whan thou comest there, I charge the, throwe my swerde in that water & come ageyn & telle me what thou there seest". "My lord," sad Bedwere, "your commaundement shal be doon & lyghtly brynge you worde ageyn." So Syr Bedwere departed & by the waye he behelde that noble swerde that the pomel & the hafte was al of precyous stones. And then he sayd to hym self, "Yf I throwe this ryche swerde in the water, therof shal neuer come good but harme and losse". And thenne Syr Bedwere hydde Excalybur vnder a tree: and so as sone as he myght he came ageyn vnto the kyng and sayd he had ben at the water & had throwen the swerde in to the water.

"What sawe thou there?" sayd the kyng. "Syr," he sayd, "I sawe no thynge but wawes & wyndes." "That is vntrewly sayd of the", sayd the kynge. "Therfore goo lyghtelye ageyn and do my commaundemente as thou arte to me leef & dere. Spare not, but throwe it in!"

SIR THOMAS MALORY, *Morte Darthur*

(*g*) And therwith the kynge awoke and was sore abasshed of this dreme and sente anone for a wyse philosopher commaundynge to telle hym the sygnyfycacion of his dreme. "Syre," sayd the philosopher, "the dragon that thow dremedest of betokeneth thyn owne persone that sayllest here & the colours of his wynges ben thy Royames that thow haste wonne: and his taylle whiche is al to tattered sygnefyeth the noble knyghtes of the round table. And the bore that the dragon slough comyng fro the clowdes betokeneth some tyraunt that tormenteth the peple or else thow arte lyke to fyghte with somme Geaunt thy self, beynge horryble and abhomynable whoos pere ye sawe

neuer in your dayes. Wherfore of this dredeful dreme doubte the
no thynge. But as a conquerour come forth thy self." Thenne
after this soone they had syghte of londe and saylled tyl they
arryued atte Barflete in Flaundres. And whanne they were there
he fond many of his grete lordes redy as they had ben com-
maunded to awayte vpon hym.

SIR THOMAS MALORY, Morte Darthur

(*b*) Certaine Spaniardes coasting alongst the Sea in search
of mines, fortuned to land in a very fertile, pleasant and well
peopled country: unto the inhabitants whereof they declared
their intent, and shewed their accustomed perswasions; saying:
That they were quiet and well-meaning men, comming from
farre-countries, being sent from the King of *Castile*, the greatest
King of the habitable earth, unto whom the Pope, representing
God on earth, had given the principality of all the *Indies*. That
if they would become tributaries to him, they should bee most
kindly used and courteously entreated: They required of them
victualles for their nourishment; and some gold for the behoofe
of certaine Physicall experiments. Moreover, they declared
unto them, the beleeving in one onely God, and the trueth of
our religion, which they perswaded them to embrace, adding
thereto some minatorie threates.

MONTAIGNE, Essays: "Of Coaches"

IX. Punctuate the following passages:

(*a*) The night was profoundly dark but the red blaze from
the New Hall which the lawless miscreants after plundering it
had fired was sufficient to enable the cavaliers to discharge their
petronels with deadly effect among the foremost of the club-
men, who were greatly superior in numbers to themselves then
rushing from their concealment with drawn swords they as-
sailed them so fiercely that the rabble-rout were panic-stricken
and after a disorderly attempt at maintaining their ground fled
precipitately in all directions

(*b*) Helen on whose startled ear the discharge of firearms
the clash of swords and the mingled yells of rage and ven-
geance had fallen in dread confusion added a faint cry of female
terror to the tumultuous din around her and sank back in a
state of utter insensibility How long her swoon continued Helen
knew not but her first sensation of consciousness was a feeling

that her peril was over for she was supported in the arms and on the bosom of some person whose form was indistinct in the surrounding darkness but whose voice of deep and tender melody as he gently soothed her with assurances that she was safe and all danger past though it had never before met her ear went to her heart like the remembered tones of some dear familiar friend

(*c*) And where am I she asked

With friends madam was the reply of her unknown protector

What friends she eagerly demanded as a sudden volume of flame from the burning mansion threw a fitful radiance over the waving plumes and lovelocks of the cavaliers

With Colonel Dagworth and a part of his regiment replied he on whose bosom she had hitherto so confidingly leaned

Colonel Dagworth she exclaimed Edward Dagworth the son of Sir Reginald Dagworth my father's enemy continued she gently struggling to disengage herself from his supporting arms is it indeed to your generous valour that I am indebted for deliverance from a fate too terrible to think upon

(*d*) She shuddered and gave way to a convulsive burst of hysterical weeping then raising her streaming eyes to his face she murmured How shall we ever repay you

I am repaid he soothingly replied richly nobly repaid by the happiness I feel in having had it in my power to perform a service for Mistress Helen Milbourne

What sweet words were these from the lips of the hero of her mental romance Insensibly her eyes closed once more and she was again supported on the manly bosom of her brave deliverer

(*a*)–(*d*). AGNES STRICKLAND, *The Love Quarrel*

(*e*) My child my own Grizel he exclaimed and she fell upon his bosom

My father my dear father sobbed the miserable maiden and she dashed away the tear that accompanied the words

Your interview must be short very short said the jailer as he turned and left them for a few minutes together

God help and comfort thee, my daughter added the unhappy father as he held her to his breast and printed a kiss upon her brow I had feared that I should die without bestowing my blessing on the head of my own child and that stung me more than death But thou art come my love thou art come and the last blessing of thy wretched father

Nay forbear forbear she exclaimed not thy last blessing not thy last My father shall not die

Be calm be calm my child returned he would to Heaven that I could comfort thee my own my own But there is no hope within three days and thou and all my little ones will be

Fatherless he would have said but the words died on his tongue

J. M. WILSON, Grizel Cochrane

(*f*) Tom Lizard told us a story the other day of some persons which our family know very well with so much humour and life that it caused a great deal of mirth at the tea-table His brother Will the Templar was highly delighted with it and the next day being with some of his Inns of Court acquaintance resolved whether out of the benevolence or the pride of his heart I will not determine to entertain them with what he called a pleasant humour enough I was in great pain for him when I heard him begin and was not at all surprised to find the company very little moved by it Will blushed looked round the room and with a forced laugh Faith gentlemen said he I do not know what makes you look so grave it was an admirable story when I heard it

SIR RICHARD STEELE, Guardian

(*g*) The Baron was going to throw the shells at his head but paused in the act and said with much dignity

Turn out the fellows pockets

But the defunct had before been subjected to the double scrutiny of Father Fothergill and the Clerk of St Bridgets It was ill gleaning after such hands there was not a single maravedi

We have already said that Sir Robert de Shurland Lord of the Isle of Sheppey and of many a fair manor on the main land was a man of worship He had rights of free-warren saccage and sockage cuisage and jambage fosse and fork infang theofe and outfang theofe and all waifs and strays belonged to him in fee simple

(*h*) Turn out his pockets said the knight

Ant please you my lord I must say as how they was turned out afore and the devil a raps left

Then bury the blackguard

Please your lordship he has been buried once

Then bury him again and be —— The Baron bestowed a benediction

The seneschal bowed low as he left the room and the Baron went on with his oysters

Scarcely ten dozen more had vanished when Periwinkle reappeared

Ant please you my lord Father Fothergill says as how that its the Grinning Sailor and he wont bury him anyhow

Oh he wont wont he said the Baron Can it be wondered at that he called for his boots

(*i*) Periwinkle said the Baron as he encased his better leg let the grave be twenty feet deep

Your lordships command is law

And Periwinkle Sir Robert stamped his left heel into its receptacle and Periwinkle see that it be wide enough to hold not exceeding two

Ye ye yes my lord

And Periwinkle tell Father Fothergill I would fain speak with his Reverence

Ye ye yes my lord

The Barons beard was peaked and his moustaches stiff and stumpy projected horizontally like those of a Tom Cat he twirled the one he stroked the other he drew the buckle of his surcingle a thought tighter and strode down the great staircase three steps at a stride

(*j*) His sword half leaped from its scabbard No the trenchant blade that had cut Suleiman Ben Malek Ben Buckskin from helmet to chine disdained to daub itself with the cerebellum of a miserable monk it leaped back again and as the Chaplain scared at its flash turned him in terror the Baron gave him a kick one kick it was but one but such a one Despite its obesity up flew his holy body in an angle of forty-five degrees then having reached its highest point of elevation sunk headlong into the open grave that yawned to receive it If the reverend gentleman had possessed such a thing as a neck he had infallibly broken it as he did not he only dislocated his vertebræ but that did quite as well He was as dead as ditch-water

In with the other rascal said the Baron and he was obeyed for there he stood in his boots Mattock and shovel made short work of it twenty feet of superincumbent mould pressed down alike the saint and the sinner Now sing a requiem who list said the Baron and his lordship went back to his oysters

(g)–(j). R. H. BARHAM ("INGOLDSBY"), Gray Dolphin

(k) Scythrop laid his pistol between his watch and his bottle The hour hand passed the VII the minute hand moved on it was within three minutes of the appointed time Scythrop called again to Crow Crow answered as before Scythrop rang the bell Raven appeared

Raven said Scythrop the clock is too fast

No indeed said Raven who knew nothing of Scythrops intentions if anything it is too slow

Villain said Scythrop pointing the pistol at him it is too fast

Yes yes too fast I meant said Raven in manifest fear

How much too fast said Scythrop

As much as you please said Raven

How much I say said Scythrop pointing the pistol again

An hour a full hour sir said the terrified butler

Put back my watch said Scythrop

T. L. PEACOCK, Nightmare Abbey

(l) He approached them and courteously inquired the way to the nearest town

There is no town within several miles was the answer

A village then if it be but large enough to furnish an inn

There is Gamwell just by but there is no inn nearer than the nearest town

An abbey then

There is no abbey nearer than the nearest inn

A house then or a cottage where I may obtain hospitality for the night

Hospitality said one of the young women you have not far to seek for that Do you not know that you are in the neighbourhood of Gamwell Hall

(m) So far from it said the knight that I never heard the name of Gamwell Hall before

Never heard of Gamwell Hall exclaimed all the young women together who could as soon have dreamed of his never having heard of the sky

Indeed no said Sir Ralph but I shall be very happy to get rid of my ignorance

And so shall I said his squire for it seems that in this case knowledge will for once be a cure for hunger wherewith I am grievously afflicted

And why are you so busy my pretty damsels weaving these garlands said the knight

Why do you not know sir said one of the young women that to-morrow is Gamwell feast

The knight was again obliged with all humility to confess his ignorance

(*l*) and (*m*).   T. L. PEACOCK, *Maid Marian*

(*n*) I followed slowly behind and entered the gate of the town an old dilapidated place consisting of little more than one street Along this street I was advancing when a man with a dirty foraging-cap on his head and holding a gun in his hand came running up to me Who are you said he in rather rough accents from whence do you come

From Badajoz and Trujillo I replied Why do you ask

I am one of the National Guard said the man and am placed here to inspect strangers I am told that a gipsy fellow just now rode through the town It is well for him that I had stepped into my house Do you come in his company

Do I look like a person said I likely to keep company with gipsies

The National measured me from top to toe and then looked me full in the face with an expression which seemed to say Likely enough In fact my appearance was by no means calculated to prepossess people in my favour

GEORGE BORROW, *The Bible in Spain*

(*o*) I dont like to see a man take his seat in the House of Lords who has not been in the House of Commons He seems to me always in a manner unfledged

It will be a long time I hope my dear father before I take my seat in the House of Lords said Lord Montacute if indeed I ever do

In the course of nature tis a certainty

Suppose the Dukes plan for perpetuating an aristocracy does not succeed said Lord Montacute and our house ceases to exist

His father shrugged his shoulders It is not our business to suppose that I hope it will never be the business of any one at least seriously This is a great country and it has become great by its aristocracy

You think then our sovereigns did nothing for our greatness Queen Elizabeth, for example of whose visit to Montacute you are so proud

They performed their part

And have ceased to exist We may have performed our part and may meet the same fate

B. DISRAELI, *Tancred*

I. Give the meanings of the words italicised in the following passage; suggest alternative words of similar meaning:

THE GRANDE CHARTREUSE

It is a fortnight since we set out hence, upon a little *excursion* to Geneva. We took the longest road which lies through Savoy, on purpose to see a famous *monastery* called the Grande Chartreuse, and had no reason to think our time lost. After having travelled seven days very slow—for we did not change horses, it being impossible for a *chaise* to go post in these roads —we arrived at a little *village* among the mountains of Savoy, called Echelles; from thence we proceeded on horses, who are used to the way, to the mountain of the Chartreuse. It is six miles to the top; the road runs *winding* up it, commonly not six feet broad; on one hand is the rock, with woods of pine trees hanging overhead; on the other, a monstrous *precipice*, almost *perpendicular*, at the bottom of which rolls a *torrent*, that some-times tumbling among the fragments of stone that have fallen from on high, and sometimes *precipitating* itself down vast descents with a noise like thunder, which is still made greater by the *echo* from the mountains on each side, concurs to form one of the most *solemn*, the most *romantic*, and the most astonish-ing scenes I ever beheld. Add to this the strange views made by the *crags* and *cliffs* on the other hand, the *cascades* that in many places throw themselves from the very summit down into the vale and the river below, and many other particulars im-possible to describe, you will conclude we had no *occasion to repent* our pains. This place St Bruno chose to retire to, and upon its very top founded the aforesaid convent, which is the *superior* of the whole order. When we came there, the two fathers who are *commissioned* to entertain strangers—for the rest must neither speak one to another, nor to any one else— received us very kindly and set before us a *repast* of dried fish, eggs, butter, and fruits, all excellent in their kind, and ex-tremely neat. They *pressed* us to spend the night there, and to stay some days with them; but this we could not do, so they led us about their house, which is, you must think, like a little *city*, for there are a hundred fathers, besides three hundred servants, that make their clothes, grind their corn, press their wine, and do everything among themselves. The whole is quite orderly and simple; nothing of *finery*; but the wonderful *decency* and the strange situation, more than supply the place of it. In the evening we *descended* by the same way, passing through many clouds that were then forming themselves on the mountain's side.

THOMAS GRAY, *Letters*

II. Make lists of words denoting different sorts of (1) ships, (2) cooking utensils, (3) artificial lights, (4) musical instruments, (5) carpentry tools.

III. Give adjectives opposite in meaning to:

shallow, false, ignorant, satisfied, narrow-minded, logical, vague, considerate, observant, powerful, accidental, permanent, scarce, fresh, orderly, amicable, dignified, distinguished, probable, offensive, awkward, artful.

IV. Give nouns opposite in meaning to:

friendship, vanity, rashness, valour, confidence, hope, delicacy, jubilation, cheerfulness, serenity, generosity, wealth, credit, acquisition, permission, liberation, success, expert, fatigue, vivacity, preservation, faith, construction.

V. Make up sentences to bring out the difference in meaning between:

council and counsel; depose and dispose; forceful and forcible; precede and proceed; relative and relation; straight and strait; stationary and stationery; young and youthful.

VI. Give adjectives and verbs corresponding to these nouns:

gold, nature, character, haste, tyrant, thief, courage, system, magnet, circle, precipice, glory.

VII. Give nouns corresponding to:

retire, accuse, speak, celebrate, promote, forge, analyse, remember, appear, invent, denounce, adopt, restore, fail, tolerate, injure, offend, persuade, intrude.

VIII. Give verbs corresponding to:

solution, satisfaction, compulsion, concession, suspicion, application, maintenance, abstinence.

IX. Give adjectives corresponding to:

theatre, fancy, muscle, plenty, saint, error, hero, joke, space, ridicule, humour, science, envy, odour, labour, irony, history, omen, legend, pope, pathos, law.

X. Give one word for each of the following phrases:

renounce an oath, on a level and facing the same way, shout of applause, charge with a fault, reverential fear, throw water out of boat, roar as a bull, recurring every two years, official numbering of population, written grant of rights by sovereign etc., draw a line round, made in imitation, worthy of belief, sail to and fro making for no particular port, reach highest point, suspended cloth used as screen, without resources, condensed account, will bend without breaking, land abutting on street or water, cover with thin layer of gold, light up, following example, bring oneself into favour with, wanting in flavour, inspire with fear, thin narrow strip of wood, one who journeys to a sacred place, moving forward, for the time being, place appointed for meeting, of inferior importance, wood prepared for building.

XI. Make lists of verbs, nouns and adjectives which could be used appropriately for each of the following subjects:

bubble, book, motor, taste, destruction, equality.

XII. What is a prefix? Give examples of words with the following prefixes:

con-, post-, sub-, mis-, re-.

XIII. What is a suffix? Illustrate your answer by reference to the following examples:

catkin, wonderful, duchess, realistic, friendship.

XIV. To what subjects would each of the adjectives in the following groups be applicable?

i. courteous, polite, civil, mannerly, well-behaved, refined.
ii. skilful, dexterous, handy, deft, proficient, expert.
iii. transparent, lucid, serene, clear, crystalline, diaphanous.
iv. plausible, servile, fulsome, soapy.

XV. Substitute a single verb for each of these expressions:

to separate grain from; pull apart; be inclined to think that; undergo pain; try hard; test the depth; draw a deep breath; start suddenly aside; make a loud cry; express dissatisfaction with; yield to pressure; become wider; keep in confinement; fill over-full; obstruct movement; announce publicly; take possession of (a house); soothe to sleep; work up into dough or paste; form an opinion; employ (person) for wages; take notice of.

XVI. Make up sentences to show how the following words are used with each of the given prepositions:

i. trust in, to, for, with.
ii. intercede with, for.
iii. board at, with, up, over, in, across.
iv. draw back, off, in, over, out, together.

XVII. Make up sentences to contain all the words in each of the following groups—one sentence for each group:

i. moment, knock, door, stranger.
ii. shadow, trees, path, darkness.
iii. smiling, anxious, inquiry, coverlet, bed.
iv. sudden, raised, listened, replaced, desk, papers, noise.
v. dreamed, led, whispering, understand, library, candle.

XVIII. Distinguish between the words in each of the following groups: illustrate with sentences that bring out the meanings:

    i. hateful, odious.
    ii. artful, artificial, fictitious.
    iii. adorn, decorate, embellish.
    iv. durable, lasting, permanent.
    v. give, grant, assign.
    vi. profit, earnings, winnings.
    vii. agreement, contract, bargain.
    viii. fatigue, weariness, lassitude.
    ix. preserve, maintain, sustain.
    x. insufficient, inadequate.
    xi. faith, trust, confidence.
    xii. edge, verge, brink, margin.
    xiii. create, fabricate, manufacture.
    xiv. resistless, invincible, impregnable.
    xv. seasonable, timely, opportune.
    xvi. early, premature, soon.
    xvii. remedy, help, redress.
    xviii. reformation, revolution, rebellion, revision.
    xix. determination, resoluteness.
    xx. disciple, follower, apostle.
    xxi. temperance, moderation, sobriety.
    xxii. regret, repentance, remorse.
    xxiii. accuser, prosecutor, plaintiff.
    xxiv. forbearance, abstinence, disuse.
    xxv. visible, perceptible, apparent.
    xxvi. distant, remote.
    xxvii. veteran, patriarch, seer.
    xxviii. spirited, spirituous, spiritual.

XIX. Re-arrange the words in each of the following groups to make complete sentences:

    i. terrace stood Erbach May long on of the ago a on Count morning.
    ii. looking away woods he over the stood silent.
    iii. castle side they to window a other the the in of along.

iv. drawbridge spurring because fall late Weissberg riders night half-score heard they hard came that to had some the the to of there.

v. reported walking ghost hat red the was as three-cornered sleeves seen with a a in and coat.

vi. gull fishermen held in Sutherland kill to of the formerly unlucky some it a.

vii. frothed a opening chin suddenly soap-lather he a shaving-cloth face to eyes the up bolted with out door with under his his.

viii. sedately right the marched turned and hand chamber but gallery to of the the into on end the dejected spectre a.

ix. animals world thoughtful the plants study every in a to been and age favourite one the of of seems have with men.

x. saw dream passing him in of which writing with his distinctly indeed were they things eye the if as mind's was he before as a he.

XX. In each of the following groups there is one word that does not belong to the series of synonyms; which is it?

i. frighten, intimidate, intimate.

ii. advise, applaud, commend, praise.

iii. check, control, urge, stop.

iv. destructive, malicious, ruinous, pernicious.

v. harbour, shelter, harmony.

vi. blame, condemn, confine, reprove.

vii. healthy, salubrious, sultry.

viii. temporary, transitory, transparent.

ix. adore, adorn, decorate, embellish.

x. doubtful, durable, dubious, uncertain.

XXI. The following list of words contains four groups of synonyms; each group consists of three words; write out the groups:

close, contest, imperfect, strict, finish, defective, rigorous, struggle, terminus, strife, severe, faulty.

XXII. Write sentences to illustrate the correct preposition after each of the following words:

contrary, different, connect, ineligible, divert, hope, rebel, attraction, accessible, acquiesce, defraud, derive, despair.

XXIII. Explain the meaning of these phrases and sentences:

he is henpecked, the story goes, out at elbows, a matter of course, an eye to business, time hanging heavily on one's hands, to the tune of, when my ship comes home, give an inch and take an ell, going a begging, in spite of one's teeth, if the worst come to the worst, left in the lurch, penny wise and pound foolish, by hook or by crook, without rhyme or reason, sink or swim, of the deepest dye, play a good knife and fork.

XXIV. Re-write the following passages substituting synonymous words for those in italics:

(a) In the midst of these *unpleasant reflections*, they *beheld* the *glittering retinue* of the emperor emerging from the great street which led then, as it still does, through the *heart* of the city. Amidst a crowd of Indian nobles, *preceded* by three officers of state bearing golden wands, they saw the royal *palanquin blazing* with burnished gold. It was borne on the shoulders of nobles, and over it a canopy of *gaudy* feather-work, *powdered* with jewels and *fringed* with silver, was supported by four *attendants* of the same rank. They were barefooted, and walked with a slow, *measured pace*, and with eyes *bent* on the ground. When the *train* had come within a *convenient* distance, it *halted*, and Montezuma, *descending* from his *litter*, came forward, leaning on the arms of the lords of Tezcuco and Iztapalapan, his nephew and brother, both of whom, as we have seen, had already been made known to the Spaniards. As the monarch *advanced* under the *canopy*, the *obsequious* attendants *strewed* the ground with cotton tapestry, that his *imperial* feet might not be *contaminated* by the *rude soil*. His subjects of high and low *degree*, who lined the sides of the *causeway*, bent forward with their eyes fastened on the ground as he *passed*, and some of the humbler *class prostrated* themselves before him. Such was the *homage* paid to the Indian *despot*, showing that the *slavish forms* of *Oriental adulation* were to be found among the *rude inhabitants* of the Western World.

W. H. PRESCOTT, *Conquest of Mexico*

(*b*) But to return to the Circus. It is *inconvenient* from its *situation*, at so great a distance from all the markets, baths, and places of *public entertainment*. The only entrance to it, through Gay Street, is so difficult, *steep*, and *slippery*, that in wet weather it must be *exceedingly dangerous*, both for those that ride in carriages, and those that walk afoot; and when the street is *covered* with snow, as it was for fifteen days *successively* this very winter, I don't see how any *individual* could go either up or down, without the most *imminent hazard* of broken *bones*. In *blowing* weather, I am told, most of the houses in this hill are *smothered* with smoke, forced down the chimneys by the gusts of wind *reverberated* from the hill behind, which (I *apprehend likewise*) must render the *atmosphere* here more *humid* and *unwholesome* than it is in the Square below: for the clouds, formed by the *constant evaporation* from the baths and rivers in the bottom, will, in their *ascent* this way, be first *attracted* and *detained* by the hill that *rises* close behind the Circus, and *load* the air with a *perpetual succession* of *vapours*. This point, however, may be easily *ascertained* by means of a hygrometer, or a paper of salt of tartar *exposed* to the *action* of the *atmosphere*.

T. SMOLLETT, *Humphrey Clinker*

(*c*) At last I began to write, and as I *finished* any *section* of my book, read it to such of my friends, as were most *skilful* in the matter which it *treated*. None of them were *satisfied*; one *disliked* the *disposition* of the parts, another the *colours* of the style; one *advised* me to *enlarge*, another to *abridge*. I *resolved* to read no more, but to take my own way and write on, for by *consultation* I only *perplexed* my thoughts and *retarded* my work.

The book was at last *finished*, and I did not doubt but my *labour* would be repaid by profit, and my *ambition satisfied* with *honours*. I *considered* that natural history is neither *temporary* nor local, and that though I *limited* my *inquiries* to my own country, yet every part of the *earth* has productions common to all the rest. *Civil* history may be *partially* studied, the revolutions of one nation may be *neglected* by another; but after that in which all have an interest, all must be *inquisitive*. No man can have *sunk* so far into *stupidity* as not to *consider* the *properties* of the *ground* on which he walks, of the *plants* on which he feeds, or the animals that *delight* his ear, or amuse his eye; and, therefore, I *computed* that *universal curiosity* would *call* for many editions of my book, and that in five years I should *gain* fifteen thousand pounds by the sale of thirty thousand copies.

SAMUEL JOHNSON, The Idler (No. 55)

(*d*) He was *apparently* a *seafaring* man, rather under the *middle size*, and with a *countenance* bronzed by a thousand *conflicts* with the north-east wind. His *frame* was *prodigiously muscular*, strong, and *thickset*, so that it seemed as if a man of much greater height would have been an *inadequate* match in any *close* personal *conflict*. He was *hard-favoured*, and, which was worse, his face *bore* nothing of the *insouciance*, the *careless, frolicsome jollity* and *vacant curiosity* of a sailor on shore. These qualities, perhaps, as much as any others, *contribute* to the *high popularity* of our seamen, and the general good *inclination* which our *society expresses* towards them. Their *gallantry, courage*, and *hardihood* are qualities which *excite reverence*, and perhaps rather *humble pacific* landsmen in their presence; and neither *respect* nor a sense of *humiliation* are feelings easily combined with a *familiar fondness* towards those who inspire them. But the *boyish frolics*, the *exulting high spirits*, the *unreflecting* mirth of a sailor when enjoying himself on shore, *temper* the more *formidable points* of his character.

SIR WALTER SCOTT, Guy Mannering

(*e*) The highest mountain crags were cleft, *in some cases*, into *fantastic* forms; single pillars stood out from all else, like *lonely watchers*, over the mountain *scene*; while little red clouds *playfully embraced* them *at intervals*, and *converted* them into pillars of fire. The sun at length *departed*, and all became cold and grey upon the mountains; but a *brief secondary glow* came afterwards, and warmed up the brown cliffs once more. I *descended* the moraine, the smell of the smoke *guiding* me towards the rock under which I was to pass the night. I stood in front of it; and, had I been a painter, I had a *capital subject*. A fire was burning at the mouth of the grotto, reddening with its glare *the darkness* of *the interior*; beside the fire sat my little companion, with a tall, conical, red night-cap drawn *completely* over his ears; our saucepan was *bubbling* on the fire; he watched it *meditatively*, adding at times a twig, which *sprung immediately* into flame, and *strengthened* the glow upon his *countenance*; he looked, in fact, more like a demon of the ice world than *a being* of ordinary flesh and blood. I had been *recommended* to take a bit of a tallow candle with me to rub my face with, as a *protection* against the sun; by the light of this we spread our rugs, lay down upon them, and wrapped them round us.

J. Tyndall, *The Glacier du Géant*

XXV. (i) Fill the blanks in the following passages with suitable adjectives, or adverbs:

(*a*) The Theatre of Puppets, or Marionetti—a   company from Milan—is, without any exception, the   exhibition I ever beheld in my life. I never saw anything so   ridiculous. They *look* between four and five feet high, but are really   smaller; for when a musician in the orchestra happens to put his hat on the stage, it becomes   gigantic, and almost blots out an actor. They usually play a comedy, and a ballet. The   man in the comedy I saw one summer night, is a waiter in an hotel. There never was such a   actor, since the world began.   pains are taken with him. He has   joints in his legs: and a practical eye, with which he winks at the pit, in a manner that is absolutely   to a stranger, but which the   audience, mainly composed of the common people, receive (so they do everything else) quite as a matter of course, and as if he were a   man. His spirits are   . He continually shakes his legs, and winks his eye. And there is a   father with   hair, who sits down on the regular   stage-bank, and blesses his daughter in the   conventional way, who is tremendous. No one would suppose it possible that anything short of a   man could be so tedious. It is the triumph of art.

C. Dickens, *Pictures from Italy*

(*b*) When the sun arose, which it did   and amidst   rain-clouds, we found ourselves in the neighbourhood of a range of mountains which lay on our left, and which, Antonio informed me, were called the Sierra of San Selvan; our route, however, lay over   plains,   clothed with brushwood, with here and there a   village, with its old and   church. Throughout the greater part of the day a drizzling rain was falling, which turned the dust of the roads into mud and mire,   impeding our progress. Towards evening we reached a moor, a   place enough, strewn with stones and rocks. Before us, at   distance, rose a conical hill, rough and   , which appeared to be neither more nor less than an   assemblage of the kind of rocks which lay upon the moor. The rain had now ceased, but a   wind rose and howled at our backs. Throughout the journey I had experienced   difficulty in keeping up with the mule of Antonio; the walk of the horse was   , and I could discover no vestige of the spirit which the Gipsy had assured me lurked within him. We were now upon a   clear spot of the moor. "I am about to see," I said, "whether this horse has any of the quality which you have described." "Do so", said Antonio, and spurred his beast onward,   leaving me far behind. I jerked the horse with the bit, endeavouring to arouse his   spirit, whereupon he stopped, reared, and refused to proceed. "Hold the bridle   , and touch him with your whip", shouted Antonio from before. I obeyed, and forthwith the animal set off at a trot, which   increased in swiftness till it became a   speedy trot.

GEORGE BORROW, The Bible in Spain

(ii) Supply suitable words for the blanks in the following passages:

(*a*) As in a mist he   a twang: he glanced down; Denys, white and   as death, was shooting up at the bear. The bear   at the twang; but   on. Again the cross-bow   ; and the bear   ; and came nearer. Again the   : and the next moment the bear was   upon Gerard, where he sat, with hair standing   on end, and eyes   from their   , palsied. The bear opened her jaws like a   ; and   blood   from them upon Gerard as from a   . The bough   . The wounded   was reeling; it clung, it stuck its sickles of   deep into the wood; it toppled, its   held   , but its body   off, and the sudden shock to the branch shook Gerard   on his stomach with his face upon one of the bear's   paws. At this, by a   effort, she raised her head up, up, till he felt her hot   breath. Then her huge teeth

together loudly close below him in the air, with a last   of
    hate. The ponderous carcass   the   out of the
bough; then pounded the earth with a   thump. There
was a shout of   below, and the very next instant a cry of
    ; for Gerard had   , and, without an attempt to save
himself, rolled   from the   height.

CHARLES READE, *The Cloister and the Hearth*

(*b*) The preacher then   into his subject like an eagle
dallying with the   . The   was upon   and war;
upon church and state—not their   but their separation—
on the spirit of the   and the spirit of Christianity, not as the
same, but as   to one another. He   of those who
had "inscribed the cross of Christ on banners   with
human   ". He made a poetical and pastoral excursion—
and to   the   effects of war, drew a   contrast
between the   shepherd   , driving his   afield, or
    under the hawthorn, piping to his   , "as though
he should never be old," and the same poor   lad, crimped,
kidnapped, brought into   , made   at an alehouse,
turned into a wretched   -boy, with his   sticking on
end with   and pomatum, a long   at his back, and
    out in the loathsome finery of the   of blood.

WILLIAM HAZLITT, *My First Acquaintance with Poets*

(*c*) I called for a   , but was for some time totally
to; which was the more   , as I could   I was the
object of curiosity to   servants, both   and   ,
from different   of the building, who   out their
heads and withdrew them, like rabbits in a   , before I
could make a direct   to the attention of any   . The
return of the   and hounds relieved me from my   ,
and with some   I got one   to relieve me of the charge
of the horses, and another stupid   to   me to the
presence of Sir Hildebrand. This   he performed with
much such grace and   , as a peasant who is compelled to
act as   to a   patrol; and in the same   I was
obliged to guard against his   me in the labyrinth of low
vaulted passages which   to "Stun Hall", as he called it,
where I was to be   to the   presence of my uncle.

SIR WALTER SCOTT, *Rob Roy*

XXVI. Study the following passages carefully and comment on appropriateness of the words used:

(a) The next day found them among the mountains, and their course became ever more difficult. Sometimes they were skirting immense precipices, sometimes their way lay over vast glaciers; then into deep valleys which but for the hardness of the snow it would have been impossible to cross. And always nearer, always louder, came that strange rumbling sound.

About midday they were traversing a narrow ledge of ice. On their right towered rocks hundreds of feet high, while on their left was a sheer fall, the bottom of which was hidden in mist and gloom. Suddenly the wall of rock turned sharply, and then a wonderful sight broke on their vision.

From the precipice, perhaps five hundred feet in height, fell an immense cascade, which, with a roar like thunder, poured down to the unseen depths beneath where they stood on that slender ledge. Roderick had read of the Falls of Niagara, but surely, he thought, they could be nothing compared with this. The cascade could not have been less than two hundred yards in width, and in that wintery sunshine, sparkled in a riot of iridescent tints, inexpressibly beautiful.

(b) During the whole period of his silent struggle to get free the street had been black and empty and deserted, but at the very moment Bill set foot on the pavement it seemed to wake into life to the wild clanging of a bell!

A brazen note—the thrilling warning note of fire—echoed in the distance, growing louder at every peal. Instinctively, despite the urgency of his own errand, Bill paused, his heart quickening at the throbbing tone, memories stirring. And then with rushing speed a powerful fire engine hurled itself round the corner and thundered overwhelmingly towards him, drenching the street with sound!

For a tense second Bill Atherton was lost to everything else —forgetful even of his own important errand. Those fire-fighters hurtling by to some distant red feast, other bells beating brazenly in the distance, all these held swiftly awakened memories—memories of adventures that had been Bill's during those last four years!

And then he pulled himself back to the urgent present, and ran with long loose strides down the street in the wake of the engine and in the direction of the house he had left four years ago.

(*c*) And so the Watcher, ever willing to oblige, made an engineer's hut some twenty miles distant his objective, and proceeded in his long, easy, tireless stride under the moss-draped trees of the valleys and along the twisting mountain tracks beetled by great peaks shouldering the stars, and below the winking lights of the village huts from whence came the scent of wood-smoke, fried cakes and rotting pine-cones—the true smell of the hills.

Long after sundown he was crossing the ravine of an aged pine forest, on the farther slopes of which he could discern the black outline of a long, wooden bungalow, its back resting against the rock mountain wall, the front supported by thick timber piles. The steps that led up to the veranda resembled the gang-plank of a ship, or stairs to the upper storey of a barn. Far above the flat, tarred roof the spacious rim of the mountain top could be seen outlined against the darkening sky, which outline was broken by the silhouettes of cranes, trucks, trolleys and loose stone heaps.

The objects gave Timber the answer for the existence of the solitary dwelling which Bernard Beavis, C.E., and one youthful assistant had housed themselves for six long, weary months while a twelve-foot roadway was being hewn out of the mountains so that a short cut could be made for the simple native village folk to bring their cattle and produce into the markets of the Simla area.

Barely had the Watcher reached the foot of the veranda steps when a cheroot was flung viciously over the rail, and while it sailed like a firefly down the hillside a short, heavily-built man creaked out of a cane chair and peered over.

(*d*) He reached the floor of the ravine, and was flitting like a shadow from tree to tree, when an agitated cry caused him to suddenly flatten himself upon the pine-cone-covered ground.

Came the vicious, reverberating crack of a revolver, the distant thudding of many bare feet, then more piercing cries; and then—silence.

The goatherd sped towards the fire, and the next minute was looking upon a sight, the like of which he had seen a few times before in his adventurous life. Only this time it was not the deserted camp of a native hillman pilgrim, robbed and perhaps left to die by blood-thirsty outlaws, but the bivouac of a British soldier who had been unexpectedly attacked, over-powered and carried away.

With steady eye he regarded the huddled horsehair blankets with a pair of black regulation boots and rolled spiral puttees neatly placed beside them; the closed novel by the valise which had served as the sleeper's pillow; a pith khaki topee; and an Army canteen filled with water.

"Jove!" he muttered, a horseshoe frown creasing his forehead.

XXVII. In the following passages select the most appropriate word from those given in brackets:

i. The (civilised, usual, ordinary) method is to (make, build, construct) a fire and then to (put, touch) a match to the (final, completed, finished) (structure, edifice, result). If (well, properly, rightly) done and in a (grate, fireplace) or stove this (acts, works, does) beautifully. Only in the woods you have no grate. The only (sure, certain, proper, true) way is as follows: (Retain, Hold, Suspend) a piece of birch (bark, rind, peel) in your hand. (Protect, Shield, Shelter) your match all you know how. When the (bark, rind, peel) has (exploded, fired, caught), lay it in your fireplace, (assist, aid, help, encourage) it with more (peel, rind, bark), and (slowly, gradually, carefully) build up, (bough, twig, branch) by (bough, twig, branch), from the (primary, preliminary, initial, first) (pin-point, spot, hint, suggestion) of flame, all the (fire, furnace, light) you are going to (use, need, require).

ii. The (referees, umpires), in long (black, white) coats, (creased, rumpled, dirty) from being (packed, stored) during the week with stumps and old bats and pads in a locker, (sauntered, ambled, strolled), (immense, great, big) with the (importance, dignity, value) of their (office, job, task), to the wickets. The (hugeness, bigness, stoutness, obesity, burliness) of Sam Bird had (caused, occasioned, made) a (tear, rent, hole) down the back of his coat, which, (as a result, in consequence) fitted him quite (easily, comfortably, loosely). As they (got to, reached, attained) the square, five Raveley men (came out, emerged, issued) from the Pavilion, and called loudly for the ball, which (new, fresh) and red and (bright, shiny, glowing) (rested, lay, reposed) in Sam's pocket.

iii. For the (rest, remainder) of the day, we (perceived, saw, recognised) no human being; we (shoved, pushed, thrust) on (eagerly, anxiously, hesitatingly) in the hope of (coming up, meeting, encountering) with the Bedouins (before, ere) (dusk, nightfall). Night (arrived, came), and we still went on in our way till about ten o'clock. Then the (complete, thorough, intense) (gloom, darkness) of the night, and the (fatigue, weariness, tiredness, lassitude) of our beasts (compelled, forced, made) us to (determine, decide) upon coming to a (standstill, halt). Upon the heights to the eastward we saw lights; these (glowed, shone) from caves on the mountain-side, (inhabited, occupied) by rascals of a low sort, from whom there was no (willing, eager, joyful) hospitality to be expected. We (caught, heard, listened to) at a little distance, the (bubbling, gurgling, brawling) of a rivulet, and on the (sides, shores, banks) of this it was determined to (make, establish, form) our bivouac; we soon found the stream, and following its (path, course, direction) for a few yards came to a (place, spot, point) which was (considered, thought, believed) (suitable, applicable, fit) for our (intention, use, purpose, habitation). It was a (very, sharply, keenly) cold night, and when I (descended, dismounted) I found myself on some wet (grass, herbage, verdure, foliage) that promised ill for our (peace, comfort, happiness).

XXVIII. Read through the nine passages on pages 76–82, and make a list of words that have changed in meaning since those passages were written; suggest modern words that could be used as substitutes.

IV. NOTE-MAKING AND PRÉCIS

I. Exercises on the five following passages:

i. Provide a title for each.
ii. Indicate where the paragraphs should begin.
iii. Give the subject of each paragraph.
iv. Summarise each passage in note form.
v. Write a short précis—in about 200 words—of each passage.

(a) That narrow strip between the high and low-water marks of spring tides which we call the sea shore is the haunt of a rich and varied collection of plants and animals and has, on account of its unique position at the junction of sea and land, an interest altogether out of proportion to its area. Many books have been written about the sea shore and its interest, but in this volume with its wider scope we can only devote one chapter to it and endeavour to give some general idea of the many fascinating problems it presents. Those who are sufficiently interested are advised to seek further information in the books recommended at the end of this volume. The extent of shore uncovered at low tide naturally depends on the sharpness of slope, and this depends on a variety of factors, the nature of the land, its configuration and the action of the tides, currents and rivers, being the most important. Anyone who has lived near the sea knows how in some places the outgoing tide uncovers great areas of mud or sand, while in others, with a quickly descending shingle beach, only a comparatively small area is uncovered at the lowest spring tides. It has been estimated that the total area between tide marks in Great Britain and Ireland amounts to some 620,000 acres. We can distinguish between three types of shore, formed of rock, sand or mud, though these may be mixed to a greater or less extent. The waves are the greatest influence at work moulding the shore, breaking with fury against the land, washing away loose material, or, with the aid of pebbles and stones which they dash against it, gradually eating into a hard, rocky coast, forming a flat "abrasion platform" at the base often of towering cliffs. Here we find a typical rocky shore. In other regions, on the other hand, the action of powerful cross currents deposits great banks of sand, formed by the breaking down of rocks. At the mouths of rivers or in sheltered creeks and gulleys there are mud flats where the sediment brought from land is deposited. The action of ice and of weathering in general also assists in the wearing away of the land and the formation of the shore, while the influence of plants and animals is not to be neglected. The former often help to bind together sand and mud and convert them into firm, dry land; encrusting animals, such as barnacles and mussels, may help to protect rocks, but usually the action of animals is destructive, notably that of the various rock borers. A feature of the greatest importance is the variability of conditions on the shore. Not only does the sea cover and uncover it twice daily, but the ranges of temperature are far greater, both yearly and often daily, than in any other part of the sea. An animal in moderately cool water at high tide may be left stranded at low tide in a small rock pool where the temperature rises to great heights under the influence of a hot summer sun. The shallow water near the shore is both warmer in summer and cooler in winter (when ice may form on the shore) than the deeper water further out. The constitution of the sea is also apt to be variable, especially near the mouths of rivers where much fresh-water is mixed with it; also in the height of summer when, in enclosed areas, evaporation may make the sea more than usually salty. The influence of light is very great, greater than in any other region except the surface waters of the open sea. This has an immediate effect in the distribution of plant life, for plants can only exist where there is light which is necessary for the "photosynthetic" action of their green pigment by means of which the carbonic acid gas in the atmosphere, or in solution, is combined with water to form starch, which, with the addition of salts obtained from the soil or from solution, forms the food of the plant. The influence of this flora of sea weeds on the life of the sea shore is of great importance. The population of the sea shore if it is to withstand these very variable conditions must be extremely hardy—how hardy we realize when we discover that very slight changes in the temperature or salinity of the water will kill animals used to the uniform conditions of the open ocean. The animals must be adapted in many different ways, for protection, food collection, and reproduction, to mention only three of the most important. Yet in spite of these difficulties the population of the sea shore is one of the densest and most varied on the surface of the earth. So dense, indeed, that the most striking features of shore life are the perpetual struggle for existence, the constant scramble for food in which the strongest or most subtle are the conquerors, innumerable devices for ensuring the continuance of the race, the never ceasing pursuit by the more powerful of the weaker and smaller, the latter surviving to the extent to which they are able to disguise or hide themselves.

F. S. RUSSELL and C. M. YONGE, *The Seas*

(*b*) No great movement in history sprang from more various motives than the Crusades. Some of these motives were not religious at all. We are here concerned with the crusades only in so far as they belong to the history of Christianity, but it is necessary to notice some of the non-religious causes, since without these the Crusades could never have taken place. It was the skill of the Papacy that turned into religious channels and used for the greater glory of the Church a variety of purely secular motives. The Crusades may be viewed as part of the age-long warfare between east and west. This warfare is as ancient as the struggle between the Greeks and the Persians and as modern as the campaigns of General Allenby in Palestine and General Maude in Mesopotamia. It is only partly religious in character. They may also be viewed as a continuation or revival of the old Viking spirit of adventure. It is notable that the Norman colonists in France and in Sicily played a leading part from the first. These were the latest and most enthusiastic converts to Christianity, and their enthusiasm expressed itself both in the architecture of their cathedrals and in the adventures of their Crusades. Again, the Crusades have an important commercial aspect. The rising Italian seaports, Venice and Genoa, wanted to open up trade with the east, and a Christian kingdom of Jerusalem stretching from the port of Joppa to the northern extremity of the Red Sea furnished them with just the sort of "Suez Canal" that they required. Indeed it may be said that religious enthusiasm, though it conquered Jerusalem, could never have held it for nearly a hundred years but for the "sinews of war" supplied by these traders for their own commercial purposes. None the less, it was religious enthusiasm that gave the Crusades their splendid and romantic character. A crusade may be defined simply as an "armed pilgrimage", a "Pilgrim's Progress" grown into a "Holy War". The idea of pilgrimage to the Holy Land had grown increasingly popular since the time when Jerome had translated the Scriptures in his monastery at Bethlehem. The Church had seized upon the idea and made pilgrimage, whether to Jerusalem or some other holy shrine, a part of its system of penances, whereby members of the Church paid the penalty for their sins, escaped the penalty of excommunication, or obtained merit in God's eyes. Pilgrimage was a popular and agreeable form of penance, combining spiritual benefits with the joys of travel. The characters in Chaucer's *Canterbury Tales* are pilgrims travelling to the shrine of St Thomas of Canterbury, but their spirit is that of holiday makers rather than penitents. (But the *Canterbury Tales* belong to a later and less religious age.) How much more popular would be a penance which afforded not only the gentle pleasures of travel but also the fiercer delights of battle with God's enemies! If the Crusader fell in battle, then the glory of one who laid down his life for his Church would certainly not be less than that of one who to-day lays down his life for his country.

D. C. SOMERVELL, *A Short History of Our Religion*

(*c*) It is safe to say that, except in the wildest and most remote corners of our island, the Fox would have been placed long ago in the list of extinct British mammals but for its careful preservation by the various "hunts". In recent times—that is since fox-hunting became a fashionable sport—the poultry and sheep-raising agriculturist has had to bear heavy losses in order that the local pack of fox-hounds may have its well-conditioned quarry at the proper season. As far back as the reign of Elizabeth an Act of Parliament was passed for the protection of grain, which incidentally provided for the payment of "xijd" for the head of every Fox or Gray that might be brought in to the officers appointed to receive them. To-day, outside the hunt areas, the killing of a Fox is considered a meritorious act, particularly in the northern mountain districts; in Cornwall, we have seen a loafer carrying a dead Fox around the villages and receiving pence from the grateful owners of domestic poultry. The head and body of the Fox measures usually a trifle over two feet in length, and the bushy, white-tipped tail adds at least another foot to his total length when running; but examples have been recorded greatly exceeding these measurements. He stands only about fourteen inches high at the shoulder. The beautiful fur is russet or red-brown above and white on the under parts. The front of the limbs and the back of the ears are black. The sharp-pointed long muzzle, the erect ears, and the quick movements of the eye with its elliptical pupil combine to give him an alert, cunning appearance, which so impressed the ancient writers that they invented many stories of his astuteness. The Foxes ("Tods") of Scotland, although of the same species, have usually greyer fur than that of the English Fox. The Fox is an ancient Briton, and he was here at a period long anterior to the Mammoth's days. The habits of the Fox are nocturnal, and save at the breeding season he leads a solitary life. The day is spent in an "earth"—a burrow underground, rarely made by himself, usually acquired from Badger or Rabbit; in the former case he has probably taken up quarters in the entrance to a Badger's earth and rendered it uninhabitable to the more cleanly beast by permeating it with the secretion from glands under the tail. In the case of the Rabbit-burrow the Fox gets undisputed possession by eating out those who constructed it. The Fox then stops all the exits except one, leaving that if possible that opens in a bramble thicket or the dense undergrowth of bracken on a hillside. From this stronghold he issues at dusk, and trots at a light easy pace along his accustomed trails, keeping a watchful eye for rabbit, hare, pheasant, partridge, hedgehog, squirrel, vole, frog—even snails and beetles. He sometimes takes to the seashore in quest of fish, crabs, and mussels. On winter nights he will prowl around the farms, looking for a hen-house whose door has not been properly secured; or for a fowl that is sleeping out in the copse. Sometimes a lamb is the victim, and in the mountain districts hunger will goad him to attack one of the small mountain sheep, especially if the vixen is hunting with him. If cornered he proves a hard fighter, and snaps like a wolf.

EDWARD STEP, *Animal Life of the British Isles*

(*d*) To make steel, it is necessary to take out part of the carbon, for, when this is done, the substance becomes tougher and less brittle. It can, when heated sufficiently, be forced into new shapes, and when cooled again be tough steel and not brittle cast iron. In order to get the excess of carbon out of the pig iron, it must be heated again to melting-point, and exposed to an atmosphere containing oxygen which will then combine with some of the carbon in the pig iron and carry it away. Up to fifty years ago this was done entirely by working the iron to and fro on a hearth over which flames were passing from the fireplace to the tall chimney. In this process the workmen have long iron rods, hooked at the ends, which they push into the furnace through small holes about six inches square. The molten slag collects on top of the liquid iron inside the furnace and has to be continually removed; the iron gets stiffer and stiffer as it is freed from carbon, and the puddler's labour becomes greater and greater, until finally he rolls together pasty balls of dazzling white iron, and removes them one by one through the furnace door. The greater part of the necessary oxygen is supplied by the lining of the furnace, which consists of oxides of iron, and is renewed after each charge. At the last stage—the making of the ball—atmospheric oxygen plays an important part. The puddler's work is very hard and trying. The iron, refined in this way, can be hammered and wrought into convenient shapes. But the method is not very satisfactory; it is nearly a century since any useful improvement was made in it. The furnace is not hot enough, and the labour too great in comparison with the output of iron. When Bessemer introduced, more than half a century ago, a far more efficient process, it quickly took the place of the older methods. In a Bessemer "converter" a powerful blast of hot air is driven through the melted iron. There is always a certain amount of silicon in the iron, and with this the oxygen of the air combines, so that the melt is made far hotter than before, and the whole operation is carried through much more effectively. The operation is even too rapid, and is better suited for making objects such as rails and girders, which need not be formed of the best steel. For the finer work there are other methods. In one of them the work is carried out on a hearth, more slowly than is possible in the Bessemer converter. The hearth is used as in the puddling process, but the hot blast gives a high temperature, and the steel is finally poured out as a mobile liquid, not pulled out in pasty lumps. Generally speaking, the more exacting are the requirements for the steel that is to be made, the more special does the furnace become, and the greater the expense required to work it. Often, too, the quantity required is not very great, and the huge furnace is replaced by a comparatively "small" furnace, which, however, may contain several tons. Such a furnace is often heated by the electric current passing between huge carbon rods. In the ordinary arc lamp the carbons are about as thick as lead pencils; in this case they are almost as thick as a man's body. It is a wonderful sight when the furnace is tipped up, and the dazzling stream of molten steel pours out into the "bucket", from which it is afterwards poured into moulds. The reduction of the amount of carbon in the cast iron from 3 or 4 per cent. to 1 per cent. or less has converted the cast iron into steel; it is not a large change in composition, but the properties of the metal have been entirely altered. It has become strong, tenacious, and malleable, and it can be welded. It now possesses the very valuable property of becoming hardened by being plunged, when heated, into a bath of cold water, oil, or other liquid. Pure iron is a very soft material; steel is iron with a small amount of carbon; cast iron is iron with a larger amount. Wrought iron from the puddler's furnace may contain as much carbon as steel, but it is called "iron"; the same product obtained from the Bessemer or other furnace is called "mild steel". The names are a little confusing to the layman.

SIR WILLIAM BRAGG, *Old Trades and New Knowledge*

(*e*) The portion of the Vatican Palace set apart for the election of the Pope, and called the Conclave, consisted of five halls or large marble rooms, two chapels, and a gallery seventy feet long. Each of these halls was divided temporarily into small apartments, running up both sides, with a broad alley between them, formed of wood, and covered with green or violet cloth. One of these apartments was assigned to each Cardinal with his attendants. The entrance to the whole of these rooms, halls, chapels, and gallery, was by a single door fastened by four locks and as many keys. As soon as the Cardinals had entered the Conclave this door was made fast, and the four keys were given to the four different orders of the city,— one to the Bishop of Rome, one to the Cardinals themselves, a third to the Roman Nobility, and the fourth to the Officer, a great noble, who kept the door. A wicket in the door, of which this Officer also kept the key, permitted the daily meals and other necessaries to be handed to the Cardinals' servants, every dish being carefully examined before it was allowed to pass in. Within the Conclave light and air were only obtained by sky-lights or windows opening upon interior courts, pre-

cluding communication from without. The gloom of the
interior was so great, that candles were burnt throughout the
Conclave at noon-day. From the moment the Conclave was
closed a silence of expectation and anxiety fell upon all Rome.
The daily life of the city was hushed. The principal thoroughfares and fortresses were kept by strong detachments of armed
troops, and the approaches to the mysterious door were
jealously watched. Men spoke everywhere in whispers, and
nothing but vague rumours of the proceedings within were
listened to in the places of public resort, and in the coteries and
gatherings of all ranks and conditions of the people. In the
interior of the Conclave, for those who were confined within its
singular seclusion, the day passed with a wearisome monotony
marked only by intrigue not less wearisome. Early in the
morning a tolled bell called the whole of its inmates to mass in
one of the small Chapels darkened with stained glass, and
lighted dimly by the tapers of the altar, and by a few wax
candles fixed in brass sockets suspended from the roof. The
Cardinals sat in stalls down either side of the Chapel, and at the
lower end was a bar, kept by the master of the ceremonies and
his assistants, behind which the attendants and servants were
allowed to stand. Mass being over, a table was placed in front
of the altar, upon which were a chalice and a silver bell. Upon
six stools near the table are seated two Cardinal-Bishops, two
Cardinal-Priests, and two Cardinal-Deacons. Every Cardinal
in his turn, upon the ringing of the bell, leaves his seat, and
having knelt before the altar in silent prayer for the guidance of
Heaven in his choice, goes round to the front of the table and
drops a paper, upon which he has written the name of a
Cardinal, into the chalice, and returns in silence to his stall. A
solemn and awful stillness pervades the scene, broken only by
the tinkling of the silver bell. The Cardinals, one by one, some
of them stalwart and haughty men, with a firm step and im-
perious glance, others old and decrepit, scarcely able to totter
from their places to the altar, or to rise from their knees without
help, advance to their mysterious choice. To the eye alone it
was in truth a solemn and impressive scene, and by a heart
instructed by the sense of sight only, the awful presence of God
the Paraclete might, in accordance with the popular belief, be
felt to hover above the Sacred Host; but in the entire assembly
to whom alone the sight was given there was probably not one
single heart to which such an idea was present. The assembly

was divided into different parties, each day by day intriguing and manœuvring, by every art of policy and every inducement of worldly interest, to add to the number of its adherents. When every Cardinal has deposited his paper, the Cardinal-Bishop takes them out of the chalice one by one, and hands them to the Cardinal-Deacon, who reads out the name of the elected, but not of the Cardinal who had placed the paper in the chalice (which is written on part of the paper so folded that even the reader does not see it); and as he reads the name, every Cardinal makes a mark upon the scroll of names he has before him. When all the names have been read, the Cardinal-Priest, from a paper which he has prepared, reads the name of him who has had the most voices and the number of the votes. If the number be more than two-thirds of the whole, the Cardinal who has received the votes is thereby elected Pope; but if not, the Cardinal-Priest rings the silver bell once more, and at the signal the master of the ceremonies advances up the Chapel, followed by a groom carrying a brazier of lighted coals, into which, in the face of the whole assembly, the papers are dropped one by one till all are consumed.

J. H. SHORTHOUSE, *John Inglesant*

II. Write a short character sketch of William III based on the following passage (about 300 words):

Thus lived and died William the Third, King of Great Britain, and Prince of Orange. He had a thin and weak body, was brown-haired, and of a clear and delicate constitution. He had a Roman eagle nose, bright and sparkling eyes, a large front, and a countenance composed to gravity and authority. All his senses were critical and exquisite. He was always asthmatical; and the dregs of the smallpox falling on his lungs, he had a constant deep cough. His behaviour was solemn and serious, seldom cheerful, and but with a few. He spoke little, and very slowly, and most commonly with a disgusting dryness, which was his character at all times, except in a day of battle; for then he was all fire, though without passion: he was then everywhere, and looked to everything. He had no great advantage from his education. De Witt's discourses were of great use to him; and he, being apprehensive of the observation of those who were looking narrowly into everything he said or did, had brought himself under a habitual caution that he could never shake off, though, in another scene, it proved as hurtful as it was then necessary to his affairs. He spoke Dutch, French, English, and German equally well; and he understood the Latin, Spanish, and Italian; so that he was well fitted to command armies composed of several nations. He had a memory that amazed all about him, for it never failed him. He was an exact observer of men and things. His strength lay rather in a true discerning and a sound judgment than in imagination or invention. His designs were always great and good; but it was thought he trusted too much to that, and that he did not descend enough to the humours of his people to make himself and his notions more acceptable to them. This, in a government that has so much of freedom in it as ours, was more necessary than he was inclined to believe. His reservedness grew on him; so that it disgusted most of those who served him: but he had observed the errors of too much talking, more than those of too cold a silence. He did not like contradiction, nor to have his actions censured; but he loved to employ and favour those who had the arts of complaisance; yet he did not love flatterers. His genius lay chiefly in war, in which his courage was more admired than his conduct. Great errors were often committed by him; but his heroical courage set things right, as it inflamed those who were about him. He was too lavish of money on some occasions, both in his buildings and to his favourites; but too sparing in rewarding services, or in encouraging those who brought intelligence. He was apt to take ill impressions of people, and these stuck long with him; but he never carried them to indecent revenges. He gave too much way to his own humour, almost in everything, not excepting that which related to his own health. He knew all foreign affairs well, and understood the state of every court in Europe very particularly. He instructed his own ministers himself; but he did not apply enough to affairs at home. He tried how he could govern us, by balancing the two parties one against another, but he came at last to be persuaded that the Tories were irreconcilable to him, and he was resolved to try and trust them no more. He believed the truth of the Christian religion very firmly, and he expressed a horror at atheism and blasphemy; and though there was much of both in his court, yet it was always denied to him and kept out of sight. He was most exemplarily decent and devout in the public exercises of the worship of God; only on week days he came too seldom to them. He was an attentive hearer of sermons, and was constant in his private prayers and in reading the Scriptures; and when he spoke of religious matters, which he did not often, it was with a becoming gravity. He was much possessed with the belief of absolute decrees: he said to me, he adhered to these because he did not see how the belief of Providence could be maintained upon any other supposition. His indifference as to the forms of church government, and his being zealous for toleration, together with his cold behaviour towards the clergy, gave them generally very ill impressions of him. In his deportment towards all about him, he seemed to make little distinction between the good and the bad, and those who served well or those who served him ill.

He loved the Dutch and was much beloved among them; but the ill returns he met from the English nation, their jealousies of him, and their perverseness towards him, had too much soured his mind, and had in a great measure alienated him from them.

G. Burnet, *History of his own Times*

III. Summarise the following passage in about 250 words:

In the middle of March of the same year (1859) we started again for a second trip on the Shire. The natives were now friendly, and readily sold us rice, fowls, and corn. We entered into amicable relations with the chief, Chibisa, whose village was about ten miles below the cataract. He had sent two men on our first visit to invite us to drink beer; but the steamer was such a terrible apparition to them, that, after shouting the invitation, they jumped ashore, and left their canoe to drift down the stream. Chibisa was a remarkably shrewd man, the very image, save his dark hue, of one of our most celebrated London actors, and the most intelligent chief, by far, in this quarter. A great deal of fighting had fallen to his lot, he said; but it was always others who began; he was invariably in the right, and they alone were to blame. He was moreover a firm believer in the divine right of kings. He was an ordinary man, he said, when his father died, and left him the chieftainship; but directly he succeeded to the high office, he was conscious of power passing into his head, and down his back; he felt it enter, and knew that he was a chief, clothed with authority, and possessed of wisdom, and people then began to fear and reverence him. He mentioned this, as one would a fact of natural history, any doubt being quite out of the question. His people, too, believed in him, for they bathed in the river without the slightest fear of crocodiles, the chief having placed a powerful medicine there which protected them from the bites of these terrible reptiles.

Leaving the vessel opposite Chibisa's village, Drs Livingstone and Kirk, and a number of the Makololo, started on foot for Lake Shirwa. They travelled in a northerly direction over a mountainous country. The people were far from being well disposed to them, and some of their guides tried to mislead them, and could not be trusted. Masakasa, a Makololo headman, overheard some remarks, which satisfied him that the guide was leading them into trouble. He was quiet till they reached a lonely spot, when he came up to Dr Livingstone, and said, "That fellow is bad, he is taking us into mischief; my spear is sharp, and there is no one here; shall I cast him into the long grass?" Had the doctor given the slightest token of assent, or even kept silence, never more would anyone have been led by that guide, for in a twinkling he would have been where "the wicked cease from troubling". It was afterwards found that in this case there was no treachery at all, but want of knowledge on their part of the language, and of the country. They asked to be led to "Nyanja Mukulu", or Great Lake, meaning by this Lake Shirwa; and the guide took them round a terribly rough piece of mountainous country, gradually edging away towards a long marsh, which from the numbers of those animals we had seen there we had called the "Elephant Marsh", but which was really the place known to him by the name "Nyanja Mukulu", or Great Lake. Nyanja or Nyanza means, generally, a marsh, lake, river, or even a mere rivulet.

The party pushed on at last without guides, or only with crazy ones, for, oddly enough, they were often under great obligations to the madmen of the different villages: one of these honoured them, as they slept in the open air, by dancing and singing at their feet the whole night. These poor fellows sympathised with the explorers, probably in the belief that they belonged to their own class; and, uninfluenced by the general opinion of their countrymen, they really pitied, and took kindly to the strangers, and often guided them faithfully from place to place, when no sane man could be hired for love or money.

The bearing of the Manganja at this time was very independent; a striking contrast to the cringing attitude they afterwards assumed, when the cruel scourge of slave-hunting passed over their country. Signals were given from the different villages by means of drums, and notes of defiance and intimidation were sounded in the travellers' ears by day; and occasionally they were kept awake the whole night, in expectation of an instant attack. Drs Livingstone and Kirk were desirous that nothing should occur to make the natives regard them as enemies; Masakasa, on the other hand, was anxious to show what he could do in the way of fighting them.

The perseverance of the party was finally crowned with success; for on the 18th of April they discovered Lake Shirwa, a considerable body of bitter water, containing leeches, fish, crocodiles, and hippopotami. From having probably no outlet, the water is slightly brackish, and it appears to be deep, with islands like hills rising out of it. Their point of view was at the base of Mount Pirimiti or Mopeu-peu, on its south-south-west side. Thence the prospect northwards ended in a sea-horizon with two small islands in the distance—a larger one, resembling a hill-top, and covered with trees, rose more in the foreground. Ranges of hills appeared on the east; and on the west stood Mount Chikala, which seems to be connected with the great mountain-mass called Zomba.

D. LIVINGSTONE, Narrative of an Expedition to the Zambesi

IV. Write a short account of Monmouth's Rebellion based on the information given in the following passage:

17th June (1685). The Duke (Monmouth) landed with but 150 men; but the whole kingdom was alarmed, fearing that the disaffected would join them, many of the trained bands flocking to him. At his landing, he published a Declaration, charging his Majesty with usurpation and several horrid crimes, on pretence of his own title, and offering to call a free Parliament. This declaration was ordered to be burnt by the hangman, the Duke proclaimed a traitor, and a reward of £5000 to any who should kill him.

At this time, the words engraved on the Monument in London, intimating that the Papists fired the City, were erased and cut out.

The exceeding drought still continues.

18*th*. I received a warrant to send out a horse with twelve days' provisions, etc.

28*th*. We had now plentiful rain after two years' excessive drought and severe winters.

Argyll taken in Scotland, and executed, and his party dispersed.

2nd July. No considerable account of the troops sent against the Duke, though great forces sent. There was a smart skirmish; but he would not be provoked to come to an encounter, but still kept in the fastnesses.

Dangerfield whipped, like Oates, for perjury.

8th July. Came news of Monmouth's utter defeat, and the next day of his being taken by Sir William Portman and Lord Lumley with the militia of their counties. It seems the Horse, commanded by Lord Grey, being newly raised and undisciplined, were not to be brought in so short a time to endure the fire, which exposed the Foot to the King's, so as when Monmouth had led the Foot in great silence and order, thinking to surprise Lieutenant-General Lord Feversham newly encamped, and given him a smart charge, interchanging both great and small shot, the Horse breaking their own ranks, Monmouth gave it over, and fled with Grey, leaving their party to be cut in pieces to the number of 2000. The whole number reported to be above 8000; the King's but 2700. The slain were most of them *Mendip-miners*, who did great execution with their tools, and sold their lives very dearly, whilst their leaders flying were pursued and taken the next morning, not far from one another. Monmouth had gone sixteen miles on foot, changing his habit for a poor coat, and was found by Lord Lumley in a dry ditch covered with fern-brakes, but without sword, pistol, or any weapon, and so might have passed for some countryman, his beard being grown so long and so gray as hardly to be known, had not his George discovered him, which was found in his pocket. It is said he trembled exceedingly all over, not able to speak. Grey was taken not far from him. Most of his party were Anabaptists and poor cloth-workers of the country, no gentlemen of account being come in to him. The arch-*boutefeu* Ferguson, Matthews, etc., were not yet found. The £5000 to be given to whoever should bring Monmouth in, was to be distributed among the militia by agreement between Sir William Portman and Lord Lumley. The battle ended, some words, first in jest, then in passion, passed between Sherrington

Talbot (a worthy gentleman, son to Sir John Talbot, and who had behaved himself very handsomely) and one Captain Love, both commanders of the militia, as to whose soldiers fought best, both drawing their swords and passing at one another. Sherrington was wounded to death on the spot, to the great regret of those who knew him. He was Sir John's only son.

9th July. Just as I was coming into the lodgings at White-hall, a little before dinner, my Lord of Devonshire standing very near his Majesty's bedchamber-door in the lobby, came Colonel Culpeper, and in a rude manner looking at my Lord in the face, asked whether this was a time and place for excluders to appear; my Lord at first took little notice of what he said, knowing him to be a hot-headed fellow, but he reiterating it, my Lord asked Culpeper whether he meant him; he said yes, he meant his Lordship. My Lord told him he was no excluder (as indeed he was not); the other affirming it again, my Lord told him he lied; on which Culpeper struck him a box on the ear, which my Lord returned, and felled him. They were soon parted, Culpeper was seized, and his Majesty, who was all the while in his bedchamber, ordered him to be carried to the Green-Cloth Officer, who sent him to the Marshalsea, as he deserved. My Lord Devon had nothing said to him.

I supped this night at Lambeth at my old friend's Mr Elias Ashmole's, with my Lady Clarendon, the Bishop of St Asaph, and Dr Tenison, when we were treated at a great feast.

JOHN EVELYN, Diary

V.   i. Summarise each of these letters in as short a form as possible without omitting any important facts.

ii. Write an account of the defeat of the Armada based on the information given in these letters.

No. 1.

Sir,   1588

I will not trouble you with any long letter; we are at this present otherwise occupied than with writing. Upon Friday, at Plymouth, I received intelligence that there were a great number of ships descried off the Lizard; whereupon, although the wind was very scant, we first warped out of harbour that night, and upon Saturday turned out very hardly, the wind

being at South-west; and about three of the clock in the afternoon, descried the Spanish fleet, and did what we could to
work for the wind, which by this morning we had recovered,
descrying their fleet to consist of 120 sail, whereof there are
four galleasses, and many ships of great burden.

At nine of the clock we gave them fight, which continued
until one. In this fight we made some of them to bear room to
stop their leaks; notwithstanding we durst not adventure to
put in among them, their fleet being so strong. But there shall
be nothing either neglected or unhazarded, that may work their
overthrow.

Sir, the captains in her majesty's ships have behaved themselves most bravely and like men hitherto, and I doubt not will
continue, to their great commendation. And so, recommending
our good success to your godly prayers, I bid you heartily
farewell. From aboard the *Ark*, thwart of Plymouth, the 21st
of July, 1588.

Your very loving friend,

C. HOWARD.

Sir, the southerly wind that brought us back from the coast
of Spain brought them out. God blessed us with turning us
back. Sir, for the love of God and our country, let us have with
some speed some great shot sent us of all bigness; for this
service will continue long; and some powder with it.

No. 2.

Right Honourable,

This bearer came aboard the ship I was in in a wonderful
good time, and brought with him as good knowledge as we
could wish. His carefulness therein is worthy recompense, for
that God has given us so good a day in forcing the enemy so
far to leeward as I hope in God the Prince of Parma and the
Duke of Sidonia shall not shake hands this few days; and
whensoever they shall meet, I believe neither of them will
greatly rejoice of this day's service. The town of Calais hath
seen some part thereof, whose mayor her majesty is beholden
unto. Business commands me to end. God bless her majesty,
our gracious sovereign, and give us all grace to live in His fear.
I assure your honour this day's service hath much appalled the

enemy, and no doubt but encouraged our army. From aboard her majesty's good ship the *Revenge*, this 29th of July 1588.

Your honour's most ready to be commanded,

FRA. DRAKE.

There must be great care taken to send us munition and victual whithersoever the enemy goeth.

Yours, FRA. DRAKE.

No. 3.

My bounden duty humbly remembered unto your good lordship:—I have not busied myself to write often to your lordship in this great cause, for that my lord admiral doth continually advertise the manner of all things that doth pass. So do others that understand the state of all things as well as myself. We met with this fleet somewhat to the westward of Plymouth upon Sunday in the morning, being the 21st of July, where we had some small fight with them in the afternoon. By the coming aboard one of the other of the Spaniards, a great ship, a Biscayan, spent her foremast and bowsprit; which was left by the fleet in the sea, and so taken up by Sir Francis Drake the next morning. The same Sunday there was, by a fire chancing by a barrel of powder, a great Biscayan spoiled and abandoned, which my lord took up and sent away.

The Tuesday following, athwart of Portland, we had a sharp and long fight with them, wherein we spent a great part of our powder and shot, so as it was not thought good to deal with them any more till that was relieved.

The Thursday following, by the occasion of the scattering of one of the great ships from the fleet, which we hoped to have cut off, there grew a hot fray, wherein some store of powder was spent; and after that little done till we came near to Calais, where the fleet of Spain anchored, and our fleet by them; and because they should not be in peace there, to refresh their water or to have conference with that of the Duke of Parma's party, my lord admiral, with firing of ships, determined to renew them; as he did, and put them to the seas; in which broil the chief galleass spoiled her rudder, and so rode ashore near the town of Calais, where she was possessed of our men, but so aground as she could not be brought away.

That morning, being Monday, the 29th of July, we followed

the Spaniards; and all that day had with them a long and great fight, wherein there was great valour showed generally of our company. In this battle there was spent very much of our powder and shot; and so the wind began to blow westerly, a fresh gale, and the Spaniards put themselves somewhat the northward, where we follow and keep company with them. In this fight there was some hurt done among the Spaniards. A great ship of the galleons of Portugal, her rudder spoiled, and so the fleet left her in the sea. I doubt not but all these things are written more at large to your lordship than I can do; but this is the substance and material matter that hath passed.

Our ships, God be thanked, have received little hurt, and are of great force to accompany them, and of such advantage that with some continuance at the seas, and sufficiently provided of shot and powder, we shall be able, with God's favour, to weary them out of the sea and confound them. Yet, as I gather certainly, there are amongst them 50 forcible and invincible ships which consist of those that follow, viz.:

Nine galleons of Portugal of 800 ton apiece, saving two of them are but 400 ton apiece.

Twenty great Venetians and argosies of the seas within the Strait, of 800 apiece.

One ship of the Duke of Florence of 800 ton.

Twenty great Biscayans of 500 or 600 ton.

Four galleasses, whereof one is in France.

There are 30 hulks, and 30 other small ships, whereof little account is to be made....

At their departing from Lisbon, the soldiers were 20,000, the mariners and others 8000; so as in all they were 28,000 men. Their commission was to confer with the Prince of Parma, as I learn, and then to proceed to the service that should be there concluded; and so the duke to return into Spain with these ships and mariners, the soldiers and their furniture being left behind. Now the fleet is here, and very forcible, and must be waited upon with all our force, which is little enough. There should be an infinite quantity of powder and shot provided, and continually sent abroad; without the which great hazard may grow to our country; for this is the greatest and strongest combination to my understanding, that ever was gathered in Christendom; therefore I wish it, of all hands, to be mightily and diligently looked unto and cared for.

... And so praying to God for a happy deliverance from the

malicious and dangerous practice of our enemies, I humbly take my leave. From the sea, aboard the *Victory*, the last of July 1588.

The Spaniards take their course for Scotland; my lord doth follow them. I doubt not, with God's favour, but we shall impeach their landing. There must be order for victual and money, powder and shot, to be sent after us.

Your lordship's humbly to command,

JOHN HAWKYNS.

VI.   Write a brief life (about 350 words) of Nansen, using the material below.

Dr Fridtjof Nansen had other claims to public recognition, but it is as an Arctic explorer of exceptional daring, initiative, and vision that he will be chiefly remembered. His two great achievements, the first crossing of Greenland, and the drift in the *Fram* across the North Polar Basin, stand out in the record of Arctic travel for boldness of conception and intrepidity of execution. Nansen was, however, much more than a bold adventurer in Arctic wastes. A skilled scientist, a publicist, a diplomat, above all an ardent patriot, he spent his later years largely in work for the relief of the distress caused by the World War.

The son of an advocate, Nansen was born on October 10, 1861, at Store Froen, near Christiania (Oslo), and educated at Christiania University. The Arctic first cast its spell over him when, as a young man of 21, poetic and impressionable in temperament, he made a voyage in the sealer *Viking* to the east coast of Greenland. From that time dated his determination to become an Arctic explorer. Meanwhile, for the six years following Nansen held the post of Curator of the Natural History Museum at Bergen. An expert ski-runner, gifted with a fine physique, he evolved his plan for crossing Greenland primarily by the use of skis, and at the age of 27 set out upon its achievement. It was denounced as foolhardy and impossible. The interior of Greenland was a *terra incognita*, peopled in the imagination of the coast Eskimos by Kivitogs, or sorcerers, whom they did not dare to face. All that was known of the heart of Greenland came from the attempt by Nordenskiold in

1883, when, attacking from the west coast, he reached an elevation of nearly 5000 ft. on a still rising snowfield.

Nansen chose the wiser plan of landing on the east coast, and pushing overland to certain succour on the west. He discarded the heavy type of sledge that imposed so much labour on earlier expeditions, and selected one of lighter build. He pinned his faith to the Norwegian ski, which later carried Amundsen by giant strides to the South Pole, and selected as his five companions the best and strongest "skilobers" he could find in Norway. They were Otto Sverdrup, a retired ship captain; Oluf Dietrichson, an Army officer; Trana, a northern peasant; and two mountain Lapps.

In mid-July, 1886, when the ship the party was in had approached within $2\frac{1}{2}$ miles of the Greenland coast, Nansen and his men took to the ice with two boats. It was Nansen's intention to steer a north-westerly course for Christianshaab, on Disco Bay, but after three weeks of arduous labour dragging the loaded sledges to the summit of the plateau at an elevation of nearly 9000 ft., he changed course and made for Godthaab, a settlement several hundred miles farther to the south, in the hope of picking up the last homeward-bound ship of the season. Once the plateau was reached the rest was comparatively easy going for a party of expert ski-runners. Difficulties increased again with the descent to sea level, but they made the head of Ameralik Fjord without accident. There Nansen and Sverdrup embarked in a crazy little boat made from willows, bamboo, and canvas, and paddled their way to the Eskimo settlement of Ny Herrnhut, near Godthaab. On October 16, two months after they left the east coast, the whole party were reunited. The story of this daring exploit was told by Nansen in *The First Crossing of Greenland*, a second volume entitled *Eskimo Life* following a few years later.

Nansen's second expedition was much more ambitious. Hitherto the main line of attack on the North Pole had been through Baffin Bay and Smith Sound—the route which ultimately yielded the great prize to Peary—and through the channel between Greenland and Spitsbergen. Meanwhile evidence had been accumulated for which there was only one explanation. There must be a hitherto unknown current across the Polar Basin from east to west, perhaps even across the Pole itself, and the theory of an Arctic continent received its first shattering blow. Nansen realized the significance of the discoveries, and on the principle that it was better to work with the forces of Nature than against them, he evolved his great plan of attempting to drift with the Poleward current. Little encouragement from British and foreign Arctic experts supported him, but Nansen held firmly to his conclusions, and the event proved their soundness.

June, 1893, saw the departure of the *Fram* from the Norwegian capital, and it was August, 1896, before she returned from the great adventure, bringing the story of one of the most remarkable voyages in Arctic history. Designed by Mr Colin Archer, the Norwegian ship-builder, the little vessel, which not only traversed the Polar Basin but later spent four winters in the Parry Archipelago and took Amundsen on his voyage for the conquest of the South Pole, was only 128 ft. over-all and 402 tons gross tonnage, but of enormous internal strength, and constructed to resist ice-packs and to raise herself under intense pressure clean on to the surface of the ice. Her captain was Otto Sverdrup, Nansen's companion on the Greenland crossing, and the whole ship's company numbered 13.

Through unexpectedly open water in the Kara Sea the *Fram* picked her way along the Siberian coast, and the high latitude of 78 deg. 43 min. had been reached before the ship was frozen in. She was then almost due north of the mouth of the Lena, and north-west of New Siberia. It was September 25, 1893, when the *Fram* entrusted herself to Nansen's theoretical Polar current, and August 13, 1896 (35 months later), when she emerged into the open waters off Spitsbergen. For three winters and three summers the ship was the sport of the elements, helpless in the grasp of the ice-fields, retreating, advancing, making angles and triangles, but slowly moving with the general drift of the pack towards the West. The *Fram* confounded the sceptics. She behaved as Colin Archer had intended, and rode safely under pressures that would have crushed to matchwood a vessel less skilfully designed.

During the second winter it became clear that the set of the current was taking the ship far south of the Pole, and Nansen resolved upon a dash northwards over the ice in the spring. The *Fram* was then almost due north of Cape Chelyuskin in lat. 84 deg. N., long. 101 deg. 55 min. E. Selecting as his sole companion Lieutenant F. H. Johansen (one of the keenest and fittest of the party), and with 28 dogs, three sledges, two kayaks,

30 days' food for the dogs, and 100 days' rations, he left the *Fram* on March 14, 1895, on one of the boldest and rashest ventures ever attempted by man. The two were alone on a boundless ocean of tumbled ice, hundreds of miles from the nearest land, and some 400 miles from their goal. Nansen was sanguine enough to hope that he might accomplish the journey and retreat on Franz Josef Land within three months, but the difficulties encountered defied the most resolute effort, and after 23 days of exhausting toil and ever-increasing obstacles, with a horizon bounded by impassable hummocks and ridges of ice, he was forced to acknowledge defeat. They had covered one-third of the distance to the Pole, but were still 260 miles from it. Their position was lat. 86 deg. 13·6 min. N., long. 95 deg. E., a new Arctic record which remained unbroken until the Italian Expedition in 1900 pushed on to 86 deg. 34 min., a little farther to the west.

When at last they made Frederick Jackson Island, it was too late in the season to attempt the contemplated desperate journey to Spitsbergen. They "dug themselves in" for the winter of 1895–6 in a small hut, and, fortunate in the abundance of walrus and bear, came safely through their third winter, with the prospect before them of another stern struggle for life in the spring. Succour was closer at hand than they suspected. Setting out again on May 19, uncertain of their whereabouts, they toiled on for another month until, on the morning of June 17, Nansen heard the bark of a dog, and saw a man approaching over the drift ice. A few minutes later he was shaking hands again and again with Mr Frederick Jackson, leader of the Jackson-Harmsworth Expedition, which had been exploring Franz Josef Land from its headquarters at Cape Flora.

On board the whaler *Windward*, the ship of Mr Jackson's expedition, Nansen and Johansen returned to Norway, and in the harbour of Tromsoe on August 21, he met the *Fram*. The little ship had broken out of the ice near Spitsbergen only a few days before, having completed her drift "according to plan", and touched lat. 85 deg. 57 min. N., an Arctic record for a vessel, and within a few miles of Nansen's farthest.

The *Fram* Expedition placed him in the front rank of Arctic explorers and brought him world-wide fame and honour. He received a special medal from the Royal Geographical Society, honorary degrees from the Universities of Oxford and Cambridge, and a gift of the *Challenger* reports from the British Government. The story is brilliantly told in Dr Nansen's *Farthest North*, published in 1897, the scientific results appearing later in a series of volumes. The explorer returned to Christiania University as Professor of Zoology, and, after taking a leading part in the movement for the separation of Norway from Sweden, he was appointed in November, 1905, Norwegian Minister in London, a post which he filled with distinction until 1908, being created G.C.V.O. in 1906. On his return to Norway he became Professor of Oceanography at the University of Christiania.

More expeditions, of a less hazardous character, followed. In 1910 Nansen cruised, making investigations into ocean currents, sea temperature, and other cognate matters, in the *Frithjof*, between Ireland and Iceland; in 1912 further oceanographic research was made in a cruise to Spitsbergen and farther north. In 1911 he had given a remarkable lecture before the Royal Geographical Society in London on the Norsemen in America.

The War period stopped exploration, but Nansen took his part in preserving the neutrality of his country, and was in 1917 sent to the United States on a mission to secure essential food supplies. After the War he became a firm supporter of the League of Nations. In the infancy of the League he rendered it useful service, and at each succeeding Assembly he was an active representative of his country. In 1920 he superintended the repatriation of War prisoners from Siberia. He was the chief inspirer and the director of the famine-relief work in Russia in 1921–23, and he was fortunate in securing, through his friendship with Mr Hoover, the active cooperation of the United States. At one time some 12,000,000 people were being fed by the organizations working under Nansen's direction. Nansen's work as High Commissioner of the League of Nations for the settlement of refugees was also of great value, and his labours on behalf of the Armenians were largely responsible for the saving of the remnant of that nation.

Notwithstanding his many other occupations, Nansen retained undiminished his interest in Polar exploration. He was one of the founders of an international society to prosecute scientific research by air, and he had planned, notwithstanding his age, to lead a party which should, from the air, make a survey—to last two years—of the North Polar Basin. For this purpose the Graf Zeppelin was engaged, and the expedition was to have started this year. But after the disaster to the Nobile expedition difficulties were encountered, and recently it was announced that the expedition had been abandoned.

In 1918 Nansen was made Rector Magnificus of Christiania University, and he was given the Nobel Peace Prize in 1922. In 1925 he was elected Rector of St Andrews University, and at his installation in November, 1926, he was given the honorary degree of LL.D. He married, in 1889, Eva, daughter of Professor Michael Sars, of Christiania. She died in 1907. In 1919 he married again, his second wife being Mme. M. S. Munthe. He had five children.

The Times, May 14, 1930

VII.   i. Supply a title for the following passage.

ii. Reduce the information to note form.

iii. Write a précis in about 200 words.

Dry air has very little chemical effect upon the materials of the earth's crust, but few rocks can stand indefinite exposure if the air be moist. Either they gradually decay, which means that some of their constituents are decomposed, or they break up without any chemical change. The decay will go on even when the water is entirely in the form of vapour, but it proceeds more rapidly and vigorously when the vapour condenses as rain or dew. The condensed vapour will not be pure water, but will always contain gases dissolved from the atmosphere, and of these oxygen and carbon dioxide are the most important aids in weathering.

Some of the chemical changes are due to the oxygen of the air, which in the presence of moisture acts powerfully upon many minerals, especially those containing iron. Basalt, for example, when exposed to the air, becomes covered with a brown crust, consisting largely of oxide of iron.

But water containing carbon dioxide appears to be the chief agent of disintegration. It dissolves carbonate of lime with comparative ease, and in course of time a limestone may be entirely removed except the clay and other insoluble matter which it usually contains. In many sandstones, the grains of sand are cemented together with carbonate of lime. This may be dissolved and the rock will then fall to pieces.

Water containing carbon dioxide acts also on other minerals. It decomposes felspar, carrying away some of its constituents in solution and leaving the rest in the form of clay. A granite may accordingly become a mass of clay with quartz and mica scattered through it. Instead of being a firm and solid rock it will then be loose and friable, and will easily be washed away.

The longer the rainwater is kept in contact with the rock the more rapid will be the disintegration. If the rock is free from pores and cracks, and its surface smooth, the rain will run off and will have little chance of causing any chemical change. But if the surface is rough and there are crevices into which the water can penetrate, it will have a longer time to produce its effects. A polished slab of granite standing vertically will resist the weather longer than a rough block lying horizontally.

The surface soil may both aid and hinder the process of decay. It acts as a sponge and keeps the rock beneath it moist after the rain has ceased. Lichens and mosses produce a similar effect and beneath a patch of moss the stone is sometimes more decayed than on the exposed surfaces. On the other hand both soil and moss impede the removal of the decayed material and so prevent the exposure of a fresh surface to the action of the weather.

Weathering due to moist air or to clinging drops of water tends to round the corners and edges of rocks and to produce convex surfaces. If we imagine a large cube of rock as made up of a number of little cubes fitted closely together, it is evident that a little cube in the middle of the side of the large cube will expose only one of its faces to the atmosphere, at an edge of the main cube it will expose two faces and at one of the corners it will expose three faces. Therefore the weathering is most rapid at the corners of the large cube, less rapid at the edges, and least rapid on the faces; and the cube becomes rounded like a cube of sugar dropped into a glass of water.

Of all the various kinds of rock the least liable to chemical change are those consisting chiefly or wholly of silica. In its crystalline form of quartz, silica is practically unaffected by water even when the water contains carbon dioxide or the acids produced by decaying vegetation. In its non-crystalline form it is soluble, but only to a very slight extent.

But even the most resistant rocks are gradually disintegrated. Changes of temperature, causing alternate expansion and contraction of the rock itself, will break up the surface. In desert

regions this is one of the most important processes of denu-
dation; but in temperate climates a much more powerful
influence is frost. No rock is absolutely impervious to water,
and when the water in the pores or crevices is frozen, it expands
and exerts great pressure upon the walls of the space in which
it is confined. By alternate thawing and freezing the cracks are
gradually enlarged and the rock is broken up. The screes or
heaps of broken rock at the foot of crags in our hilly districts
are due chiefly to this cause.

LAKE, *Physical Geography*

VIII. i. Supply a title for the following passage.

ii. Write a précis of it in about 250 words.

Another, and important, consideration that emerges from a
study of man's past history on this planet is that of human
progress. There are, of course, some people who take a pessi-
mistic view of man's progress. They point to the rise and fall
of the great civilisations of the past, such as those of Egypt,
Greece and Rome, and argue from this that the history of man
does not show any marked, and sustained, progress. But, apart
from the fact that, in many ways, we have advanced since the
days of the Egyptians, and the Greeks, and the Romans, to
take these civilisations as a base-line in arriving at a conclusion
as to whether man has progressed or not is an entirely mis-
leading procedure. To be able to reach a correct decision upon
this matter, it is vitally necessary to take the long view, and to
adopt as a base-line the very earliest human beings, who were
but little removed from an animal state, and whose highest
mechanical achievement was a piece of flint, roughly chipped
into a simple implemental form. The antiquity of these people,
as compared with that of the civilisations of Egypt, Greece, and
Rome, is profound, and dates back, probably, to a time sepa-
rated from the present by not far short of 1,000,000 years. When
we proceed to compare these most ancient flint implements
with the mechanical achievements of the present day, we see
that in this form of human endeavour the advance has been
enormous. Again, when we consider what must have been the
state of these people just emerging from an animal condition,
we know that, with all the lack of perfection in human affairs
at the present day, we have, nevertheless, attained to a develop-

ment of intellect, and morality, using this term in its widest sense, which, without any doubt, is infinitely in advance of that of Pliocene man. In fact, it may be said with truth that even the man in the street of to-day would have been regarded by his earliest ancestors as possessed of almost god-like powers and influence. It is, of course, necessary to realise that the vehicle of human progress has not followed an uninterrupted forward course. Sometimes it has stopped, occasionally it has gone back, but, when a comparison is made of the attainments and conditions of the first human beings with those of civilised races of the twentieth century, the only real basis for such a comparison, then no doubt can be entertained as to the reality, and the extent, of the progress that has been made. But, though this is the case, and though man has advanced some way upon his difficult evolutionary path, yet it must not be imagined that he has attained, nor anything like attained, to the summit of his destiny. Geologically speaking the human race is but a late comer on this planet, and even with all its present achievements is still only, as it were, upon the threshold. Man is always endeavouring to get into closer touch with and to establish control over his environment, but this power cannot be achieved quickly; it is bound to be a gradual process, but as it goes on, so will his lot in this world become more and more pleasant. The evidence of the certain, though slow, as is the case with most natural developments, progress of the human race over a period of, probably, 1,000,000 years seems to point to the operation of some at present undefined law of human progress which, as it has operated in the past, will go on functioning in the future. He would be a bold man who would venture to predict what will be the achievements of the human race in the remote future. But, if the present rate of progress is maintained, even the next few hundred years will witness an astounding change in man's whole environment, and it may be taken for granted that the present state of things will be then regarded in the same way as we regard, for instance, the condition of affairs existing in the Early Middle Ages. In these matters it is particularly needful to have a correct perspective, and the only thing that can give us this is a knowledge of the past history of mankind. The researches into this history which have been carried out by archaeologists all over the world are unfolding a truly majestic story of man's gradual ascent from the lowliest beginnings—to an ever-increasing height of attainment. We see him, in the dim days of the Pliocene, gifted with but little intellect, and armed only with sticks and stones, fighting for his existence with great and powerful animal enemies. We see him surviving the onset of arctic cold—and, as better conditions obtained, coming back to his old haunts and with undiminished courage taking up the struggle of life. And it is well to remember that, while without thought we may be inclined to look with contempt upon these primitive people of the past, yet, but for their triumphant, though enormously difficult, fight for survival we would not be in existence to-day. These are some of the things that a study of early man teaches. It teaches us to be philosophic, and to realise that the present is but a phase in an immense history that extends back into the remote past, and, so far as we can see, will extend into an equally remote future. It is destructive of the idea that "We are the people, and wisdom will die with us". Man is not engaged in a hopeless conflict with his environment—a weary swinging of the pendulum between advancement and retrogression—but from his earliest days has progressed, and, there is every reason to believe, will continue to do so in the future. That, in my judgment, is one of the most important lessons to be learned from prehistoric archaeology.

REID MOIR, *Antiquity of Man in East Anglia*

V. PARAPHRASE

I. Re-write the nine passages that follow in modern English, using words and constructions with which you are familiar. Do not follow the originals too closely.

(a)   *To my right worshipful Mother,*
               Margaret Paston, at Mawteby.

(Between 1470 and 1474)

Right Worshipful Mother, after all humble recommendations, as lowly as I can, I beseech you of your blessing.

Please you to weet that late yester night I came to Norwich, purposing to have been at this day with you at Mawteby, but it is so that I may not hold my purpose, for he that shall pay me my quarter wages for me and my retinue is in Norwich, and waiteth hourly when his money shall come to him. It is one Edmund Bowen of the Exchequer, a special friend of mine, and he adviseth me to tarry till the money be come, lest that I be unpaid, "for who cometh first to the mill, first must grind".

And as I was writing this bill, one of the grooms of my lord's chamber came to me, and told me that my lady will be here in Norwich tomorrow at night towards Walsingham, which shall, I wot well, be another let to me, but I had more need to be otherwise occupied than to await on ladies, for there is as yet, I trow, no spear that shall go over the sea so evil horsed as I am, but it is told me that Richard Calle hath a good horse to sell, and one John Butcher of Oxborough hath another, and if it might please you to give Sym leave to ride into that country at my cost, and in your name, saying that ye will give one of your sons a horse, desiring him that he will give you a pennyworth for a penny, and he shall, and the price be reasonable, hold him pleased with your payment out of my purse, though he know it not ere his horse depart from his hands. Mother, I beseech you, and it may please you to give Sym leave to ride on this message in your name that he may be here with me tomorrow in the morning betimes, for were I once horsed, I trow I were as far forth ready as some of my neighbours.

I heard a little word that ye purposed to be here in Norwich the next week, I pray God it be this week.

Mother, I beseech you that I may have an answer tomorrow at the farthest of this matter and of any other service that it please you to command me, which I will at all seasons (be) ready to accomplish with God's grace, whom I beseech to preserve you and yours.

Written at Norwich, this Wednesday in Easter week.

By your son and servant,

JOHN PASTON.

(b) I trow God did never give more grace and fortune to any people than he did as then to this gentle knight Sir John of Hainault and to his company. For these English archers intended to none other thing, but to murder and rob them, for all that they were come to serve the King in his business. These strangers were never in so great peril all the season that they lay, nor were they ever after in surety till they were again at Wissant in their own country. For they were fallen in so great hate with all the archers of the host, that some of the barons and knights of England showed unto the lords of Hainault, giving them warning that the archers and other of the common people were allied together to the number of six thousand, to the intent to burn or to kill them in their lodgings either by night or by day. So they lived at a hard adventure; but each of them promised to help and aid other, and to sell dearly their lives or they were slain. So they made many fair ordinances among themselves by good and great advice, whereby they were fain oftentimes to lie in their harness by night, and in the day to keep their lodgings, and to have all their harness ready and their horses saddled. Thus continually they were fain to make watch by their constables in the fields and highways about the court, and to send out scout-watches a mile off to see if ever any such people were coming to themward, as they were informed of; to the intent that if their scout-watch heard any noise or moving of people drawing to the cityward, then incontinent they should give them knowledge, whereby they might the sooner gather together, each of them under his own banner, in a certain place the which they had advised for the same intent. In this tribulation they abode in the suburbs by the space of four weeks, and all that season they durst not go far from their harness, nor from their lodgings, saving certain of the chief lords among them, which went to the court to see the King and his Council, who made them right good cheer.

BERNERS' translation of FROISSART's *Chronicles* (1523)

(*c*) Anon after the death of the pope Gregory, the cardinals drew them into the conclave, in the palace of Saint Peter. Anon after, as they were entered to choose a pope, according to their usage, such one as should be good and profitable for holy Church, the Romans assembled them together in a great number and came into the bowrage of Saint Peter: they were to the number of thirty thousand what one and other, in the intent to do evil, if the matter went not according to their appetites. And they came oftentimes before the conclave, and said, Hark ye, sir cardinals, deliver you at once, and make a pope; ye tarry too long; if ye make a Roman, we will not change him; but if ye make any other, the Roman people and consuls will not take him for pope, and ye put yourself all in adventure to be slain. The cardinals, who were as then in the danger of the Romans, and heard well those words, they were not at their ease, nor assured of their lives, and so appeased them of their ire as well as they might with fair words; but so much rose the felony of the Romans, that such as were next to the conclave, to the intent to make the cardinals afraid, and to cause them to condescend the rather to their opinions, brake up the door of the conclave whereas the cardinals were. Then the cardinals went surely to have been slain, and so fled away to save their lives, some one way and some another; but the Romans were not so content, but took them, and put them together again, whether they would or not. The cardinals then seeing themselves in the danger of the Romans, and in great peril of their lives, agreed among themselves, more for to please the people than for any devotion; howbeit, by good election they chose an holy man, a cardinal of the Roman nation, whom Pope Urban the Fifth had made cardinal, and he was called before, the Cardinal of Saint Peter. This election pleased greatly the Romans, and so this good man had all the rights that belonged to the papality: howbeit he lived not but three days after, and I shall show you why. The Romans, who desired a pope of their own nation, were so joyful of this new pope, that they took him, who was a hundred year of age, and set him on a white mule, and so led him up and down through the city of Rome, exalting him, and showing how they had vanquished the cardinals, seeing they had a pope Roman according to their own intents, in so much that the good holy man was so sore travailed that he fell sick, and so died the third day, and was buried in the Church of Saint Peter, and there he lieth.

BERNERS' translation of FROISSART's *Chronicles* (1523)

(*d*) (i) Now we went merrily before the wind with all the sails we could bear, insomuch that in the space of twenty-four hours, we sailed near 47 leagues, that is, seven score English miles, betwixt Friday at noon and Saturday at noon (notwithstanding the ship was very foul, and much grown with being long at sea) which caused some of our company to make account they would see what running at tilt there should be at Whitehall upon the Queen's Day. Others were imagining what a Christmas they would keep in England with their shares of the prizes we had taken.

But so it befell that we kept a cold Christmas with the Bishop and his Clerks (rocks that lie to the westwards from Scilly and the western parts of England), for soon after, the wind scanting, came about to the eastwards (the worst part of the heavens for us, from which the wind could blow) in such sort, that we could not fetch any part of England.

And hereupon also, our allowance of drink, which was scant enough before, was yet more scanted, because of the scarcity thereof in the ship. So that now a man was allowed but half a pint at a meal, and that many times cold water, and scarce sweet.

(ii) "There I had occasion", said he, "to go to many countries of every side. For there was no ship ready to any voyage or journey but I and my fellows were into it very gladly received." The ships that they found first were made plain, flat and broad in the bottom, trough-wise. The sails were made of great rushes, or of wickers, and in some places of leather. Afterward they found ships with ridged keels, and sails of canvas, yea and, shortly after, having all things like ours: the shipmen also very expert and cunning, both in the sea and in the weather. But he said that he found great favour and friendship among them for teaching them the feat and the use of the lodestone, which to them before that time was unknown. And

therefore they were wont to be very timorous and fearful upon
the sea, not to venture upon it but only in the summer time.
But now they have such a confidence in that stone that they
fear not stormy winter: in so doing farther from care than
danger; insomuch that it is greatly to be doubted lest that thing,
through their own foolish hardiness, shall turn them to evil
and harm, which at the first was supposed should be to them
good and commodious.

ROBINSON's translation of SIR THOMAS MORE's *Utopia* (1551)

(*e*) Those towns that we call thoroughfares have great and
sumptuous inns builded in them, for the receiving of such
travellers and strangers as pass to and fro. The manner of
harbouring wherein is not like to that of some other countries,
in which the host or goodman of the house doth challenge a
lordly authority over his guests, but clean otherwise, since
every man may use his inn as his own house in England, and
have for his money how great or how little variety of victuals,
and what other service himself shall think expedient to call for.
Our inns are also very well furnished, with napery, bedding,
and tapestry, especially with napery; for beside the linen used
at the tables, which is commonly washed daily, is such and so
much as belongeth unto the estate and calling of the guest.
Each comer is sure to lie in clean sheets, wherein no man hath
been lodged since they came from the laundress, or out of the
water wherein they were last washed. If the traveller have an
horse, his bed doth cost him nothing, but if he go on foot, he
is sure to pay a penny for the same; but whether he be horse-
man or footman, if his chamber be once appointed, he may
carry the key with him, as of his own house, so long as he
lodgeth here. If he lose ought whilst he abideth in the inn, the
host is bound by a general custom to restore the damage, so
that there is no greater security anywhere for travellers than
in the greatest inns of England. Their horses in like sort are
walked, dressed and looked unto by certain hostlers or hired
servants, appointed at the charges of the goodman of the house,
who in hope of extraordinary reward will deal very diligently
after outward appearance in this their function and calling.
Herein, nevertheless, are many of them blameworthy, in that
they do not only deceive the beast oftentimes of his allowance
by sundry means, except their owners look well to them, but
also make such packs with slipper merchants which hunt after
prey (for what place is sure from evil and wicked persons?)

that many an honest man is spoiled of his goods as he travelleth to and fro, in which feat also the counsel of the tapsters or drawers of drink, and chamberlains, is not seldom behind or wanting.

R. HOLINSHED, Chronicles (1577)

(*f*) (i) The King of England, to the end the peace might be fully concluded, came and encamped within half a league of Amiens. The king was at the gate, from whence he might behold the Englishmen afar off as they came. To say the truth, they seemed but young soldiers, for they rode in very evil order. The king sent to the King of England three hundred carts laden with the best wines that might be gotten, the which carriage seemed afar off almost as great as the King of England's army. Many Englishmen, because of the truce, repaired to the town, where they behaved themselves very indiscreetly, and without all regard of their prince's honour. They came all in arms, and in great troops; and if the king our master would have dealt falsely with them, so great a number might never so easily have been destroyed. Notwithstanding, he meant nothing less, but studied to make them good cheer, and to conclude a sure peace with them for his time.

(ii) He had caused to be set at the entry of the town gate two long tables, on each side of the street one, furnished with all kind of delicate meats that provoke drink, and with the best wines that might be gotten, and men to wait upon them; of water there was no mention. At each of these tables he had placed five or six great fat gentlemen of good houses, thereby the better to content those that desired to drink. The gentlemen's names were these: Monsieur de Cran, de Briqueler, de Bresmes, de Villiers, and others. So soon as the Englishmen drew near the gate, they might behold this good cheer. Besides this, men purposely appointed took their horses by the bridles, saying that they would break a staff with them, and so led them to the table, where they were feasted according to the variety of the meats, which they took in very good part. After they were within the town, what house soever they entered into they paid nothing. Further, nine or ten taverns were well furnished at the king's charge of all things necessary, whither they went to eat and drink, and call for what they would, but the king defrayed all; and this cheer endured three or four days.

THOMAS DANETT's translation of PHILIP DE COMMINES' Memoirs (1596) (*g*) Now for the services of the sea, they are innumerable: it is the great purveyor of the world's commodities to our use, conveyer of the excess of rivers, uniter by traffic of all nations: it presents the eye with the diversified colours and motions, and is, as it were with rich brooches, adorned with various islands: it is an open field for merchandise in peace; a pitched field for the most dreadful fights of war; yields diversity of fish and fowl for diet, materials for wealth, medicine for health, simples for medicines, pearls and other jewels for ornament, amber and ambergrise for delight, the wonders of the Lord in the deep for instruction, variety of creatures for use, multiplicity of natures for contemplation, diversity of accidents for admiration, compendiousness to the way, to full bodies healthful evacuation, to the thirsty earth fertile moisture, to distant friends pleasant meeting, to weary persons delightful refreshing, to studious and religious minds a map of knowledge, mystery of temperance, exercise of continence, school of prayer, meditation, devotion, and sobriety; refuge to the distressed, portage to the merchant, passage to the traveller, customs to the prince, springs, lakes, rivers, to the earth; it hath on it tempests and calms to chastise the sins, to exercise the faith, of seamen; manifold affections in itself, to affect and stupefy the subtlest philosopher; sustaineth movable fortresses for the soldier; maintaineth (as in our island) a wall of defence and watery garrison to guard the state; entertains the sun with vapours, the moon with obsequiousness, the stars also with a natural looking-glass, the sky with clouds, the air with temperateness, the soil with suppleness, the rivers with tides, the hills with moisture, the valleys with fertility; containeth most diversified matter for meteors, most multiform shapes, most various, numerous kinds, most immense, difformed, deformed, unformed monsters; once (for why should I longer detain you?) the sea yields action to the body, meditation to the mind, the world to the world, all parts thereof to each part, by this art of arts, navigation.

S. PURCHAS, *His Pilgrimage* (1613)

(*h*) To the Reverend Dr Greenwood, Vice-Chancellor of the University of Oxford, and other Members of the Convocation.

Edinburgh, 4th Feb. 1650.

Honoured Gentlemen,

I have received, by the hands of those worthy Persons of your University sent by you into Scotland, a Testimony of very high respect and honour, in your choosing me to be your Chancellor. Which deserves a fuller return, of deep resentment, value, and acknowledgement, than I am any ways able to make. Only give me leave a little to expostulate on your and my own behalf. I confess it was in your freedom to elect, and it would be very uningenious in me to reflect upon your action; only (though somewhat late) let me advise you of my unfitness to answer the ends of so great a Service and Obligation, with some things very obvious.

I suppose a principal aim in such elections hath not only respected abilities and interest to serve you, but freedom as to opportunities of time and place. As the first may not be well supposed, so the want of the latter may well become me to represent to you. You know where Providence hath placed me for the present; and to what I am related if this call were off,—I being tied to attendance in another Land as much out of the way of serving you as this, for some certain time yet to come appointed by the Parliament. The known esteem and honour of this place is such, that I should wrong it and your favour very much, and your freedom in choosing me, if, either by pretended modesty or in any unbenign way, I should dispute the acceptance of it. Only I hope it will not be imputed to me as a neglect towards you, that I cannot serve you in the measure I desire.

I offer these exceptions with all candour and clearness to you, as leaving you most free to mend your choice in case you think them reasonable; and shall not reckon myself the less obliged to do all good offices for the University. But if these prevail not, and that I must continue this honour,—until I can personally serve you, you shall not want my prayers That that seed and stock of Piety and Learning so marvellously springing up amongst you, may be useful to that great and glorious Kingdom of our Lord Jesus Christ; of the approach of which so plentiful an effusion of the Spirit upon those hopeful plants is one of the best presages. And in all other things I shall, by the

Divine assistance, improve my poor abilities and interests in manifesting myself, to the University and yourselves,

Your most cordial friend and servant,

OLIVER CROMWELL.

(*i*) He (Mr Hampden) was a gentleman of a good family in Buckinghamshire, and born to a fair fortune, and of a most civil and affable deportment. In his entrance into the world, he indulged to himself all the licence in sports and exercises, and company, which was used by men of the most jolly conversation. Afterwards, he retired to a more reserved and melancholy society, yet preserving his own natural cheerfulness and vivacity, and above all, a flowing courtesy to all men; though they who conversed nearly with him, found him growing into a dislike of the ecclesiastical government of the church, yet most believed it rather a dislike of some churchmen, and of some introducements of theirs, which he apprehended might disquiet the public peace. He was rather of reputation in his own country, than of public discourse, or fame in the kingdom, before the business of ship-money: but then he grew the argument of all tongues, every man inquiring who and what he was, that durst, at his own charge, support the liberty and property of the kingdom, and rescue his country, as he thought, from being made a prey to the court. His carriage, throughout this agitation, was with that rare temper and modesty, that they who watched him narrowly to find some advantage against his person, to make him less resolute in his cause, were compelled to give him a just testimony. And the judgement that was given against him infinitely more advanced him, than the service for which it was given. When this parliament began (being returned knight of the shire for the county where he lived), the eyes of all men were fixed on him, as their *patriae pater*, and the pilot that must steer the vessel through the tempests and rocks which threatened it. And I am persuaded, his power and interest, at that time, was greater to do good or hurt, than any man's in the kingdom, or than any man of his rank hath had in any time: for his reputation of honesty was universal, and his affections seemed so publicly guided, that no corrupt or private ends could bias them.

CLARENDON's *History of the Rebellion* (1707)

II. Write down the substance of the following passages of verse in your own language. Do not follow the originals too closely either as regards wording, or arrangement.

(a) What I shall leave thee, none can tell,
But all shall say I wish thee well:
I wish thee, Vin, before all wealth,
Both bodily and ghostly health;
Nor too much wealth nor wit come to thee,
So much of either may undo thee.
I wish thee learning not for show,
Enough for to instruct and know;
Not such as gentlemen require
To prate at table or at fire.
I wish thee all thy mother's graces,
Thy father's fortunes and his places.
I wish thee friends, and one at court,
Not to build on, but support;
To keep thee not in doing many
Oppressions, but from suffering any.
I wish thee peace in all thy ways,
Nor lazy nor contentious days;
And, when thy soul and body part,
As innocent as now thou art.

R. CORBET, *To Vincent Corbet*

(b) Behind the footlights hangs the rusty baize,
A trifle shabby in the upturned blaze
Of flaring gas, and curious eyes that gaze.
The stage, methinks, perhaps is none too wide
And hardly fit for royal Richard's stride,
Or Falstaff's bulk, or Denmark's youthful pride.
Ah, well! no passion walks its humble boards;
O'er it no king nor valiant Hector lords:
The simplest skill is all its space affords.
The song and jest, the dance and trifling play,
The local hit at follies of the day,
The trick to pass an idle hour away,—
For these, no trumpets that announce the Moor,
No blast that makes the hero's welcome sure,—
A single fiddle in the overture!

BRET HARTE

(*c*) Dost thou not blush, pernicious Catiline,
Or hath the paleness of thy guilt drunk up
Thy blood, and drawn thy veins as dry of that,
As is thy heart of truth, thy breast of virtue?
Whither at length wilt thou abuse our patience?
Still shall thy fury mock us! to what license
Dares thy unbridled boldness run itself!
Do all the nightly guards kept in the palace,
The city's watches, with the people's fears,
The concourse of all good men, this so strong
And fortifièd seat here of the senate,
The present looks upon thee, strike thee nothing?
Dost thou not feel thy counsels all laid open,
And see thy wild conspiracy bound in
With each man's knowledge? Which of all this order
Canst thou think ignorant, if they will but utter
Their conscience to the right, of what thou didst
Last night, what on the former, where thou wert,
Whom thou didst call together, what thy plots were?
O, age and manners! this the consul sees,
The senate understands, yet this man lives!—
Lives! ay, comes here into council with us,
Partakes the public cares, and with his eye
Marks and points out each man of us to slaughter.
And we, good men, do satisfy the state,
If we can shun but this man's sword and madness.
There was that virtue once in Rome, when good men
Would, with more sharp coercion, have restrained
A wicked citizen, than the deadliest foe.
We have that law still, Catiline, for thee;
An act as grave as sharp: the state's not wanting,
Nor the authority of this senate; we,
We that are consuls, only fail ourselves.

BEN JONSON, *Catiline*

(*d*) Who from the top of his prosperities
Can take a fall, and yet without surprise;
Who with the same august and even state
Can entertain the best and worst of fate;
Whose suffering's sweet, if honour once adorn it;
Who slights revenge, yet does not fear, but scorn it;
Whose happiness in every fortune lives,
For that no fortune either takes or gives;

Who no unhandsome ways can bribe his fate,
Nay out of prison marches through the gate;
Who, losing all his titles and his pelf,
Nay, all the world, can never lose himself;
This person shines indeed; and he that can
Be virtuous is the great immortal man.

KATHERINE PHILIPS, *The Virtuous Man*

(*e*) What is the end of Fame? 'tis but to fill
     A certain portion of uncertain paper:
Some liken it to climbing up a hill,
     Whose summit, like all hills, is lost in vapour;
For this men write, speak, preach, and heroes kill,
     And bards burn what they call their "midnight taper",
To have, when the original is dust,
A name, a wretched picture, and worse bust.

What are the hopes of man? Old Egypt's king
     Cheops erected the first pyramid
And largest, thinking it was just the thing
     To keep his memory whole, and mummy hid;
But somebody or other rummaging,
     Burglariously broke his coffin's lid:
Let not a monument give you or me hopes,
Since not a pinch of dust remains of Cheops.

But I being fond of true philosophy,
     Say very often to myself, "Alas!
All things that have been born were born to die,
     And flesh (which Death mows down to hay) is grass;
You've pass'd your youth not so unpleasantly,
     And if you had it o'er again—'twould pass—
So thank your stars that matters are no worse,
And read your Bible, sir, and mind your purse".

LORD BYRON

(*f*)   On what foundation stands the warrior's pride,
How just his hopes, let Swedish Charles decide;
A frame of adamant, a soul of fire,
No dangers fright him, and no labours tire;
O'er love, o'er fear, extends his wide domain,
Unconquered lord of pleasure and of pain;
No joys to him pacific sceptres yield,
War sounds the trump, he rushes to the field;

Behold surrounding kings their power combine,
And one capitulate, and one resign;
Peace courts his hand, but spreads her charms in vain;
"Think nothing gain'd", he cries, "till nought remain,
On Moscow's walls till Gothic standards fly,
And all be mine beneath the polar sky".
The march begins in military state,
And nations on his eye suspended wait;
Stern famine guards the solitary coast,
And winter barricades the realms of frost;
He comes; nor want, nor cold, his course delay;
Hide, blushing glory, hide Pultowa's day!
The vanquish'd hero leaves his broken bands,
And shews his miseries in distant lands;
Condemn'd a needy supplicant to wait,
While ladies interpose, and slaves debate.
But did not chance at length her error mend?
Did no subverted empire mark his end?
Did rival monarchs give the fatal wound?
Or hostile millions press him to the ground?
His fall was destin'd to a foreign strand,
A petty fortress, and a dubious hand;
He left the name at which the world grew pale,
To point a moral, or adorn a tale.

SAMUEL JOHNSON, *Vanity of Human Wishes*

(g) All human things are subject to decay
And, when Fate summons, monarchs must obey.
This Flecknoe found, who, like Augustus, young
Was called to empire and had governed long,
In prose and verse was owned without dispute
Through all the realms of Nonsense absolute.
This aged prince, now flourishing in peace
And blessed with issue of a large increase,
Worn out with business, did at length debate
To settle the succession of the state;
And pondering which of all his sons was fit
To reign and wage immortal war with wit,
Cried, "'Tis resolved, for Nature pleads that he
Should only rule who most resembles me.
Shadwell alone my perfect image bears,
Mature in dullness from his tender years.

Shadwell alone of all my sons is he
Who stands confirmed in all stupidity.
The rest to some faint meaning make pretence,
But Shadwell never deviates into sense.
Some beams of wit on other souls may fall,
Strike through and make a lucid interval;
But Shadwell's genuine night admits no ray,
His rising fogs prevail upon the day."

JOHN DRYDEN, *MacFlecknoe*

(*b*)   Beside yon straggling fence that skirts the way,
With blossomed furze unprofitably gay,
There, in his noisy mansion, skilled to rule,
The village master taught his little school;
A man severe he was, and stern to view,
I knew him well, and every truant knew;
Well had the boding tremblers learnt to trace
The day's disasters in his morning face;
Full well they laughed with counterfeited glee
At all his jokes, for many a joke had he;
Full well the busy whisper circling round,
Conveyed the dismal tidings when he frowned;
Yet he was kind, or, if severe in aught,
The love he bore to learning was in fault;
The village all declared how much he knew;
'Twas certain he could write and cypher too;
Lands he could measure, terms and tides presage,
And even the story ran—that he could gauge;
In arguing, too, the parson owned his skill,
For even though vanquished, he could argue still;
While words of learned length and thundering sound
Amazed the gazing rustics ranged around,
And still they gazed, and still the wonder grew,
That one small head could carry all he knew.

OLIVER GOLDSMITH, *The Deserted Village*

(*i*) His talk was like a stream, which runs
        With rapid change from rocks to roses;
    It slipped from politics to puns,
        It passed from Mahomet to Moses;

Beginning with the laws which keep
    The planets in their radiant courses,
And ending with some precept deep
    For dressing eels, or shoeing horses.

His sermon never said or showed
    That Earth is foul, that Heaven is gracious,
Without refreshment on the road
    From Jerome, or from Athanasius:
And sure a righteous zeal inspired
    The hand and head that penned and planned them,
For all who understood admired,
    And some who did not understand them.

He did not think all mischief fair,
    Although he had a knack of joking;
He did not make himself a bear,
    Although he had a taste for smoking;
And when religious sects ran mad,
    He held, in spite of all his learning,
That if a man's belief is bad,
    It will not be improved by burning.

WINTHROP MACKWORTH PRAED, The Vicar

(j) To my true king I offered, free from stain,
    Courage and faith; vain faith, and courage vain.
    For him I threw lands, honours, wealth, away,
    And one dear hope, that was more prized than they.
    For him I languished in a foreign clime,
    Grey-haired with sorrow in my manhood's prime;
    Heard on Lavernia Scargill's whispering trees,
    And pined by Arno for my lovelier Tees;
    Beheld each night my home in fevered sleep,
    Each morning started from the dream to weep;
    Till God, who saw me tried too sorely, gave
    The resting-place I asked, an early grave.
    O thou, whom chance leads to this nameless stone,
    From that proud country which was once mine own,
    By those white cliffs I never more must see,
    By that dear language which I spake like thee,
    Forget all feuds, and shed one English tear
    O'er English dust. A broken heart lies here.

LORD MACAULAY, A Jacobite's Epitaph

(k)   That place, that does contain
My books, the best companions, is to me
A glorious court, where hourly I converse
With the old sages and philosophers.
And sometimes, for variety, I confer
With kings and emperors, and weigh their counsels;
Calling their victories, if injustly got,
Unto a strict account: and in my fancy,
Deface their ill-planned statues. Can I then
Part with such constant pleasures, to embrace
Uncertain vanities? No: be it your care
To augment your heap of wealth; it shall be mine
To increase in knowledge. Lights there for my study!

J. FLETCHER, *The Elder Brother*

(l)   He lived in that past Georgian day,
When men were less inclined to say
That "Time is Gold", and overlay
        With toil their pleasure;
He held some land, and dwelt thereon,—
Where, I forget,—the house is gone;
His Christian name, I think, was John,—
        His surname, Leisure.

Reynolds has painted him,—a face
Filled with a fine, old-fashioned grace,
Fresh coloured, frank, with ne'er a trace
        Of trouble shaded;
The eyes are blue, the hair is drest
In plainest way,—one hand is prest
Deep in a flapped canary vest,
        With buds brocaded.

He wears a brown old Brunswick coat,
With silver buttons,—round his throat,
A soft cravat;—in all you note
        An elder fashion,—
A strangeness, which, to us who shine
In shapely hats,—whose coats combine
All harmonies of hue and line,—
        Inspires compassion.

AUSTIN DOBSON, *A Gentleman of the Old School*

VI. STUDY OF PROSE PASSAGES

(*a*)   To J. B. DIBDIN.

P.M. September 9, 1826.

An answer is requested.

Saturday.

Dear D.—I have observed that a Letter is never more acceptable than when received upon a rainy day, especially a rainy Sunday; which moves me to send you somewhat, however short. This will find you sitting after Breakfast, which you will have prolonged as far as you can with consistency to the poor handmaid that has the reversion of the Tea Leaves; making two nibbles of your last morsel of *stale* roll (you cannot have hot new ones on the Sabbath), and reluctantly coming to an end, because when that is done, what can you do till dinner? You cannot go to the Beach, for the rain is drowning the sea, turning rank Thetis fresh, taking the brine out of Neptune's pickles, while mermaids sit upon rocks with umbrellas, their ivory combs sheathed for spoiling in the wet of waters foreign to them. You cannot go to the library, for it's shut. You cannot cast accounts, for your ledger is being eaten up with moths in the Ancient Jewry. You cannot play at draughts, for there is none to play with you, and besides there is not a draught board in the house. You cannot go to market, for it closed last night. You cannot look in the shops, their backs are shut upon you. You cannot while away an hour with a friend, for you have no friend round that Wrekin. You cannot divert yourself with a stray acquaintance, for you have picked none up. You cannot bear the chiming of Bells, for they invite you to a banquet, where you are no visitant. You cannot cheer yourself with the prospect of a tomorrow's letter, for none come on Mondays. You cannot count those endless vials on the mantlepiece with any hope of making a variation in their numbers. You have counted your spiders; your Bastille is exhausted. You sit and deliberately curse your hard exile from all familiar sights and sounds. Any thing to deliver you from this intolerable weight of Ennui. You are too ill to shake it off: not ill enough to submit to it, and to lie down as a lamb under it. The Tyranny of Sickness is nothing to the Cruelty of Convalescence: 'tis to have Thirty Tyrants for one. That pattering rain drops on your brain. You'll be worse after dinner, for you must dine at one to-day, that Betty may go to afternoon service. She insists upon having her chopped hay. And then when she goes out, who *was* something to you, something to speak to—what an interminable afternoon you'll have to go thro'. You can't break yourself from your locality: you cannot say "Tomorrow morning I set off for Banstead": for you are book'd for Wednesday. Foreseeing this, I thought a *cheerful letter* would come in opportunely. If any of the little topics for mirth I have thought upon should serve you in this utter extinguishment of sunshine, to make you a little merry, I shall have had my ends. I love to make things comfortable. [*Here is an erasure.*] This, which is scratch'd out, was the most material thing I had to say, but on maturer thoughts I defer it.

P.S.—We are just sitting down to dinner with a pleasant party, Coleridge, Reynolds the dramatist, and Sam Bloxam; tomorrow (that is, to*day*), Liston, and Wyat of the Wells, dine with us. May this find you as jolly and freakish as we mean to be.   C. LAMB.

  i. Write out any words and phrases in the above that would not be used in the same way now.

 ii. What do you know of Neptune, the Bastille, and Coleridge?

iii. Write four more thoughts for a gloomy day beginning, "You cannot..."

 iv. What effect on his reader did Charles Lamb hope to produce with this letter?

  v. Does the letter suggest anything to you about the character of Charles Lamb?

 vi. Write a reply either in a facetious strain, or in a peevish manner.

vii. Write a short composition on the subject, "Occupations for a rainy day".

viii. Write the kind of letter you would like to receive when convalescent.

(*b*) March 9th. 1666. Made a visit to the Duke of Albemarle, and to my great joy find him the same man to me that
heretofore, which I was in great doubt of, through my negli-
gence in not visiting of him a great while; and having now set
all to rights there, I shall never suffer matters to run so far
backwards again as I have done of late, with reference to my
neglecting him and Sir W. Coventry. The truth is, I do indulge
myself a little the more in pleasure, knowing that this is the
proper age of my life to do it; and out of my observation that
most men that do thrive in the world, do forget to take pleasure
during the time that they are getting their estate, but reserve
that till they have got one, and then it is too late for them to
enjoy it.

15th. To Hales, where I met my wife and people; and do find
the picture, above all things, a most pretty picture, and mighty
like my wife; and I asked him his price: he says 14*l.* and the
truth is, I think he do deserve it.

17th. To Hales's, and paid him 14*l.* for the picture, and 1*l.* 5*s.*
for the frame. This day I began to sit, and he will make me, I
think, a very fine picture. He promises it shall be as good as
my wife's, and I sit to have it full of shadows, and do almost
break my neck looking over my shoulder to make the posture
for him to work by. Home, having a great cold: so to bed,
drinking butter-ale.

19th. After dinner we walked to the King's playhouse, all
in dirt, they being altering of the stage to make it wider. But
God knows when they will begin to act again; but my business
here was to see the inside of the stage and all the tiring-rooms
and machines: and, indeed, it was a sight worthy seeing. But
to see their clothes, and the various sorts, and what a mixture
of things there was; here a wooden-leg, there a ruff, here a
hobby-horse, there a crown, would make a man split himself
with laughing; and particularly Lacy's wardrobe, and Shotrell's.
But then again, to think how fine they show on the stage by
candle-light, and how poor things they are to look at too near
hand, is not pleasant at all. The machines are fine, and the
paintings very pretty. With Sir W. Warren, talking of many
things belonging to us particularly, and I hope to get something considerably by him before the year be over. He gives
me good advice of circumspection in my place, which I am
now in great mind to improve; for I think our office stands on
very ticklish terms, the Parliament likely to sit shortly and

likely to be asked more money, and we able to give a very bad account of the expense of what we have done with what they did give before.

28th. To the Cockpit, and dined with a great deal of company at the Duke of Albemarle's, and a bad and dirty, nasty dinner. This night, I am told, the Queen of Portugal, the mother to our Queen, is lately dead and news brought of it hither this day.

30th. I out to Lombard-street, and there received 2200*l.* and brought it home; and, contrary to expectation, received 35*l.* for the use of 2000*l.* of it for a quarter of a year, where it hath produced me this profit, and hath been a convenience to me as to care and security at my house, and demandable at two days' warning, as this hath been.

Pepys' Diary

   i. Re-write the first entry in this Diary in a short sentence.

  ii. What impression do these extracts give you of the character of Samuel Pepys (1633–1703)?

 iii. Describe a visit you have made to a building still under construction.

 iv. Write out some extracts from your (imaginary) Diary.

  v. Write a short composition with the title "Behind the Scenes".

 vi. Write a letter to a friend describing how you sat for your portrait.

 vii. Write a letter to an artist telling him that you think his portrait of your father is a poor piece of work, and that the price is exorbitant.

viii. Write out six good reasons for not having your portrait painted.

(*c*) I was travelling in a stage coach with three male Quakers, buttoned up in the straitest non-conformity of their sect. We stopped to bait at Andover, where a meal, partly tea apparatus, partly supper, was set before us. My friends confined themselves to the tea-table. I in my way took supper. When the landlady brought in the bill, the eldest of my companions discovered that she had charged for both meals. This was resisted. Mine hostess was very clamorous and positive. Some mild arguments were used on the part of the Quakers, for which the heated mind of the good lady seemed by no means a fit recipient. The guard came in with his usual peremptory notice. The Quakers pulled out their money, and formally tendered it—so much for tea—I, in humble imitation, tendering mine—for the supper which I had taken. She would not relax in her demand. So they all three quietly put up their silver, as did myself, and marched out of the room, the eldest and gravest going first, with myself closing up the rear, who thought I could not do better than follow the example of such grave and warrantable personages. We got in. The steps went up. The coach drove off. The murmurs of mine hostess, not very indistinctly or ambiguously pronounced, became after a time inaudible—and now my conscience, which the whimsical scene had for a time suspended, beginning to give some twitches, I waited, in the hope that some justification would be offered by these serious persons for the seeming injustice of their conduct. To my great surprise, not a syllable was dropped on the subject. They sat as mute as at a meeting. At length the eldest of them broke silence, by inquiring of his next neighbour, "Hast thee heard how indigos go at the India House?" and the question operated as a soporific on my moral feeling as far as Exeter.

CHARLES LAMB, *Imperfect Sympathies*

    i. Give the meaning of: straitest, to bait, recipient, peremptory, formally, ambiguously, inaudible, soporific.

   ii. What justification, if any, do you think could be given for the behaviour of the three Quakers?

  iii. Write an account of the incident as it might have been related by one of the other travellers.

  iv. Charles Lamb relates this episode to illustrate one of the characteristics of the Quaker; what was it?

   v. Invent another incident to illustrate the same characteristic, *or* its opposite.

  vi. Write a short composition describing anything of interest that has happened to you during a railway journey.

vii. Write a comparison between travelling by coach and travelling by railway train.

(d) For several hours I urged forward my beast at a rapid though steady pace, but now the pangs of thirst began to torment me. I did not relax my pace, however, and I had not suffered long when a moving object appeared in the distance before me. The intervening space was soon traversed, and I found myself approaching a Bedouin Arab mounted on a camel, attended by another Bedouin on foot. They stopped. I saw that, as usual, there hung from the pack-saddle of the camel a large skin water-flask, which seemed to be well filled. I steered my dromedary close up alongside of the mounted Bedouin, caused my beast to kneel down, then alighted, and keeping the end of the halter in my hand, went up to the mounted Bedouin without speaking, took hold of his water-flask, opened it, and drank long and deep from its leathern lips. Both of the Bedouins stood fast in amazement and mute horror; and really, if they had never happened to see an European before, the apparition was enough to startle them. To see for the first time a coat and a waistcoat, with the semblance of a white human head at the top, and for this ghastly figure to come swiftly out of the horizon upon a fleet dromedary, approach them silently and with a demoniacal smile, and drink a deep draught from their water-flask—this was enough to make the Bedouins stare a little; they, in fact, stared a great deal—not as Europeans stare, with a restless and puzzled expression of countenance, but with features all fixed and rigid, and with still, glassy eyes. Before they had time to get decomposed from their state of petrifaction I had remounted my dromedary, and was darting away towards the east.

A. W. KINGLAKE, *Eothen*

i. Suggest a short title for this passage.
ii. Give alternative expressions for: the intervening space was soon traversed; the apparition was enough to startle them; decomposed from their state of petrifaction; darting away towards the east.
iii. What do you know about Bedouins, camels and dromedaries?
iv. Describe the incident as related by one of the Arabs.

v. Invent another incident of a similar character but to take place in England.

vi. Write a short composition on "Desert travelling".

(e) The wind was blowing hard towards the shore, if that can be called a shore which consists of steep abrupt precipices, on which the surf was breaking with the noise of thunder, tossing up clouds of spray and foam to the height of a cathedral. We coasted slowly along, rounding several tall forelands, some of them piled up by the hand of nature in the most fantastic shapes. About nightfall Cape Finisterre was not far ahead,— a bluff, brown, granite mountain, whose frowning head may be seen far away by those who traverse the ocean. The stream which poured round its breast was terrific, and though our engines plied with all their force, we made little or no way.

By about eight o'clock at night the wind had increased to a hurricane, the thunder rolled frightfully, and the only light which we had to guide us on our way was the red forked lightning, which burst at times from the bosom of the big black clouds which lowered over our heads. We were exerting ourselves to the utmost to weather the cape, which we could descry by the lightning on our lee, its brow being frequently brilliantly lighted up by the flashes which quivered around it, when suddenly, with a great crash, the engine broke, and the paddles, on which depended our lives, ceased to play.

I will not attempt to depict the scene of horror and confusion which ensued; it may be imagined, but never described. The captain, to give him his due, displayed the utmost coolness and intrepidity. He and the whole crew made the greatest exertions to repair the engine, and when they found their labour in vain, endeavoured, by hoisting the sails, and by practising all possible manœuvres, to preserve the ship from impending destruction. But all was of no avail; we were hard on a lee shore, to which the howling tempest was impelling us. About this time I was standing near the helm, and I asked the steersman if there was any hope of saving the vessel, or our lives. He replied, "Sir, it is a bad affair. No boat could live for a minute in this sea, and in less than an hour the ship will have her broadside on Finisterre, where the strongest man-of-war ever built must go to shivers instantly—None of us will see the morning".

The captain, likewise, informed the other passengers in the cabin to the same effect, telling them to prepare themselves; and having done so, he ordered the door to be fastened, and none to be permitted to come on deck. I, however, kept my station, though almost drowned with water, immense waves continually breaking over our windward side and flooding the ship. The water casks broke from their lashings, and one of them struck me down, and crushed the foot of the unfortunate man at the helm, whose place was instantly taken by the captain. We were now close to the rocks, when a horrid convulsion of the elements took place. The lightning enveloped us as with a mantle, the thunders were louder than the roar of a million cannon, the dregs of the ocean seemed to be cast up, and in the midst of all this turmoil, the wind, without the slightest intimation, *veered right about*, and pushed us from the horrible coast faster than it had previously driven us towards it.

GEORGE BORROW, *The Bible in Spain*

  i. Supply a title.
 ii. Make a list of nouns used for winds of different forces; and a list of adjectives applicable to winds.
iii. Pick out the phrase or sentence that gives the most vivid impression of danger.
 iv. Explain the meanings of these phrases: the hand of nature; lowered over our heads; to give him his due; on a lee shore; the dregs of the ocean; veered right about.
  v. Describe the feeling of relief experienced when the wind "veered right about".
 vi. Make a list of any other good descriptions of storms that you have read.
vii. Describe the worst thunderstorm you can remember.
viii. Write a short story entitled, "At the eleventh hour".

(*f*) Looking now to the right, I suddenly became aware that high above us, a multitude of crags and leaning columns of ice, on the stability of which we could not for an instant calculate, covered the precipitous incline. We were not long without an illustration of the peril of our situation. We had reached a position where massive ice-cliffs protected us on one side, while in front of us was a space more open than any we had yet passed; the reason being that the ice avalanches had chosen it for their principal path. We had just stepped upon this space when a peal above us brought us to a stand. Crash! crash! crash! nearer and nearer, the sound becoming more continuous and confused, as the descending masses broke into smaller blocks. Onward they came! boulders half a ton and more in weight, leaping down with a kind of maniacal fury, as if their sole mission was to crush the séracs[1] to powder. Some of them on striking the ice rebounded like elastic balls, described parabolas through the air, again madly smote the ice, and scattered its dust like clouds in the atmosphere. Some blocks were deflected by the collision with the glacier, and were carried past us within a few yards of the spot where we stood. I had never before witnessed an exhibition of force at all comparable to this, and its proximity rendered that fearful which at a little distance would have been sublime.

My companion held his breath for a time, and then exclaimed, "C'est terrible! il faut retourner". In fact, while the avalanche continued we could not at all calculate upon our safety. When we heard the first peal we had instinctively retreated to the shelter of the ice bastions; but what if one of these missiles struck the tower beside us! would it be able to withstand the shock? We knew not. In reply to the proposal of my companion, I simply said, "By all means, if you desire it; but let us wait a little". I felt that fear was just as bad a counsellor as rashness, and thought it but fair to wait until my companion's terror had subsided. We waited accordingly, and he seemed to gather courage and assurance. I scanned the heights and saw that a little more effort in an upward direction would place us in a much less perilous position, as far as the avalanches were concerned. I pointed this out to my companion, and we went forward. Once indeed, for a minute or two, I felt anxious. We had to cross in the shadow of a tower of ice, of a loose and threatening character, which quite overhung our track. The freshly broken masses at its base, and at some distance below it, showed that it must have partially given way some hours before. "Don't speak, or make any noise", said my companion; and, although rather sceptical as to the influence of speech in such a case, I held my tongue and

[1] ice-towers.

escaped from the dangerous vicinity as fast as my legs and alpenstock could carry me.

J. TYNDALL, *The Glacier du Géan*

i. Supply a suitable title.

ii. Give synonyms and antonyms for each of the following words: stability, massive, confused, maniacal, subsided, assurance, scanned, threatening, partially, sceptical, vicinity.

iii. Consider whether any of the synonyms given in the last answer would be more suitable than the words actually used in the extract.

iv. Suggest other sights that would be fearful in proximity, but sublime at a little distance.

v. Does this passage throw any light on the character of the writer?

vi. Which do you think is the more effective simile, "the ice rebounded like elastic balls", or "(the ice) scattered its dust like clouds"?

vii. Describe the incident from the point of view of the writer's companion.

viii. Write an account of the most thrilling experience you have had.

(*g*) On the morning of the 31st of May, the families of the London citizens were stirring early in all houses. From Temple Bar to the Tower, the streets were fresh strewed with gravel, the footpaths were railed off along the whole distance, and occupied on one side by the guilds, their workmen, and apprentices, on the other by the city constables and officials in their gaudy uniforms, "with their staves in hand for to cause the people to keep good room and order". Cornhill and Gracechurch Street had dressed their fronts in scarlet and crimson, in arras and tapestry, and the rich carpet-work from Persia and the East. Cheapside, to outshine her rivals, was draped even more splendidly in cloth of gold, and tissue, and velvet. The sheriffs were pacing up and down on their great Flemish horses, hung with liveries, and all the windows were thronged with ladies crowding to see the procession pass. At length the Tower guns opened, the grim gates rolled back, and under the archway in the bright May sunshine, the long column began slowly to defile. Two states only permitted their representatives to grace the scene with their presence—Venice and France. It was, perhaps, to make the most of this isolated countenance, that the French ambassador's train formed the van of the cavalcade. Twelve French knights came riding foremost in surcoats of blue velvet with sleeves of yellow silk, their horses trapped in blue, with white crosses powdered on their hangings. After them followed a troop of English gentlemen, two and two, and then the Knights of the Bath, "in gowns of violet, with hoods purfled with miniver like doctors". Next, perhaps at a little interval, the abbots passed on, mitred, in their robes; the barons followed in crimson velvet, the bishops then, and then the earls and marquises, the dresses of each order increasing in elaborate gorgeousness. All these rode on in pairs. Then came alone Audeley, lord-chancellor, and behind him the Venetian ambassador and the Archbishop of York; the Archbishop of Canterbury, and Du Bellay, Bishop of Bayonne and of Paris, not now with bugle and hunting-frock, but solemn with stole and crozier. Next, the lord mayor, with the city mace in hand, the Garter in his coat of arms; and then Lord William Howard—Belted Will Howard, of the Scottish Border, Marshal of England. The officers of the queen's household succeeded the marshal in scarlet and gold, and the van of the procession was closed by the Duke of Suffolk, as high constable, with his silver wand. It is no easy matter to picture to ourselves the blazing trail of splendour which in such a pageant must have drawn along the London streets,—those streets which now we know so black and smoke-grimed, themselves then radiant with masses of colour, gold, and crimson, and violet. Yet there it was, and there the sun could shine upon it, and tens of thousands of eyes were gazing on the scene out of the crowded lattices.

Glorious as the spectacle was, perhaps however, it passed unheeded. Those eyes were watching all for another object, which now drew near. In an open space behind the constable there was seen approaching "a white-chariot", drawn by two palfreys in white damask which swept the ground, a golden canopy borne above it making music with silver bells: and in the chariot sat the observed of all observers, the beautiful occasion of all this glittering homage; fortune's plaything of the hour, the Queen of England[1]—queen at last—borne along upon the waves of this sea of glory, breathing the perfumed incense of greatness which she had risked her fair name, her delicacy, her honour, her self-respect, to win; and she had won it.

J. A. FROUDE, *Henry VIII*

i. Pick out words and phrases in this passage that give an impression of colour.

ii. Consider the appropriateness of these phrases: "the blazing trail of splendour", "radiant with masses of colour", "glittering homage", "perfumed incense of greatness".

iii. What do you know of, Temple Bar, the Tower, surcoat, hangings, mitred, stole and crozier, lattices, damask, canopy, Garter?

iv. Summarise the passage in about fifty words, and supply a title.

v. Compare the street decorations here described with those customary in these days.

vi. Write a description of any procession you have seen.

(*b*) It was about the year 1688 that the word stockjobber was first heard in London. In the space of four years a crowd of companies, every one of which confidently held out to subscribers the hope of immense gains, sprang into existence: the Insurance Company, the Paper Company, the Lute-string Company, the Pearl Fishery Company, the Glass Bottle Company, the Alum Company, the Blythe Coal Company, the Swordblade Company. There was a Tapestry Company, which would soon furnish pretty hangings for all the parlours of the middle class and for all the bedchambers of the higher. There was a Copper Company, which proposed to explore the mines of England, and held out a hope that they would prove not less valuable than those of Potosi. There was a Diving Company, which undertook to bring up precious effects from shipwrecked vessels, and which announced that it had laid in a stock of wonderful machines resembling complete suits of armour. In front of the helmet was a huge glass eye, like that of Polyphemus; and out of the crest went a pipe, through which

[1] Anne Boleyn.

the air was to be admitted. The whole process was exhibited on the Thames. Fine gentlemen and fine ladies were invited to the show, were hospitably regaled, and were delighted by seeing the divers in their panoply descend into the river, and return laden with old iron and ship's tackle. There was a Greenland Fishing Company, which could not fail to drive the Dutch whalers and herring busses out of the Northern Ocean. There was a Tanning Company, which promised to furnish leather superior to the best that was brought from Turkey or Russia. There was a society which undertook the office of giving gentlemen a liberal education on low terms, and which assumed the sounding name of the Royal Academies Company. In a pompous advertisement it was announced that the directors of the Royal Academies Company had engaged the best masters in every branch of knowledge, and were about to issue twenty thousand tickets at twenty shillings each. There was to be a lottery: two thousand prizes were to be drawn; and the fortunate holders of the prizes were to be taught, at the charge of the Company, Latin, Greek, Hebrew, French, Spanish, conic sections, trigonometry, heraldry, japanning, fortification, book-keeping, and the art of playing the theorbo. Some of these companies took large mansions, and printed their advertisements in gilded letters. Others, less ostentatious, were content with ink, and met at coffee-houses in the neighbourhood of the Royal Exchange. Jonathan's and Garraway's were in a constant ferment with brokers, buyers, sellers, meetings of directors, meetings of proprietors. Time bargains soon came into fashion. Extensive combinations were formed, and monstrous fables were circulated, for the purpose of raising or depressing the shares. Our country witnessed for the first time those phenomena with which a long experience has made us familiar. A mania of which the symptoms were essentially the same with those of the mania of 1720, of the mania of 1825, of the mania of 1845, seized the public mind. An impatience to be rich, a contempt for those slow but sure gains which are the proper reward of industry, patience, and thrift, spread through society. The spirit of the cogging dicers of Whitefriars took possession of the grave senators of the city, wardens of trades, deputies, aldermen. It was much easier and much more lucrative to put forth a lying prospectus announcing a new stock, to persuade ignorant people that the dividends could not fall short of twenty per cent., and to part with five thousand pounds of this imaginary wealth for ten thousand solid guineas, than to load a ship with a well-chosen cargo for Virginia or the Levant. Every day some new bubble was puffed into existence, rose buoyant, shone bright, burst, and was forgotten.

LORD MACAULAY, *History of England*

i. Supply an appropriate title for this passage.

ii. Look up in a Dictionary the origins of these words: busses, japanning, theorbo, cogging, buoyant, senators.

iii. Invent three more Companies and give particulars of their activities.

iv. Summarise this passage in about fifty words.

v. Write some extracts from the diary of a man who had invested £100 in the Diving Company.

vi. Write a short prospectus for the Royal Academies Company.

(*i*) The deep projection of the second story gave the house such a meditative look, that you could not pass it without the idea that it had secrets to keep, and an eventful history to moralize upon. In front, just on the edge of the unpaved sidewalk, grew the Pyncheon-elm, which, in reference to such trees as one usually meets with, might well be termed gigantic. It had been planted by a great-grandson of the first Pyncheon, and, though now fourscore years of age, or perhaps nearer a hundred, was still in its strong and broad maturity, throwing its shadow from side to side of the street, overtopping the seven gables, and sweeping the whole black roof with its pendent foliage. It gave beauty to the old edifice, and seemed to make it a part of nature. The street having been widened about forty years ago, the front gable was now precisely on a line with it. On either side extended a ruinous wooden fence, of open lattice-work, through which could be seen a grassy yard, and, especially in the angles of the building, an enormous fertility of burdocks, with leaves, it is hardly an exaggeration to say, two or three feet long. Behind the house there appeared to be a garden, which undoubtedly had once been extensive, but was now infringed upon by other enclosures, or shut in by habitations and out-buildings that stood on another street. It would be an omission, trifling indeed, but unpardonable, were we to forget the green moss that had long since gathered over the projections of the windows, and on the slopes of the roof; nor must we fail to direct the reader's eye to a crop, not of weeds, but flower-shrubs, which were growing aloft in the air, not a great way from the chimney, in the nook between two of the gables. They were called Alice's Posies. The tradition was, that a certain Alice Pyncheon had flung up the seeds in sport, and that the dust of the street and the decay of the roof gradually formed a kind of soil for them, out of which they grew, when Alice had long been in her grave. However the flowers might have come there, it was both sad and sweet to observe how nature adopted to herself this desolate, decaying, gusty, rusty old house of the Pyncheon family; and how the ever-returning summer did her best to gladden it with tender beauty and grew melancholy in the effort.

NATHANIEL HAWTHORNE, *The House of the Seven Gables*

   i. Pick out words and phrases in this passage that suggest age.
  ii. Give the meanings of: meditative, moralize, maturity, pendent, fertility, infringed, desolate, decaying, melancholy.
iii. Make a rough sketch of the picture suggested by this passage.
 iv. Describe any old house that you know.
  v. Write an autobiography of an old house.
 vi. Invent another story to account for the presence of the flower-shrubs growing between the two gables.

(*j*) This is the history of Silas Marner, until the fifteenth year after he came to Raveloe. The livelong day he sat in his loom, his ear filled with its monotony, his eyes bent close down on the slow growth of sameness in the brownish web, his muscles moving with such even repetition that their pause seemed almost as much a constraint as the holding of his breath. But at night came his revelry: at night he closed his shutters, and made fast his doors, and drew forth his gold. Long ago the heap of coins had become too large for the iron pot to hold them, and he had made for them two thick leather bags, which wasted no room in their resting-place, but lent themselves

flexibly to every corner. How the guineas shone as they came
pouring out of the dark leather mouths! The silver bore no
large proportion in amount to the gold, because the long pieces
of linen which formed his chief work were always partly paid
for in gold, and out of the silver he supplied his own bodily
wants, choosing always the shillings and sixpences to spend in
this way. He loved the guineas best, but he would not change
the silver—the crowns and half-crowns that were his own
earnings, begotten by his labour; he loved them all. He spread
them out in heaps and bathed his hands in them; then he
counted them and set them up in regular piles, and felt their
rounded outline between his thumb and fingers, and thought
fondly of the guineas that were only half earned by the work in
his loom, as if they had been unborn children—thought of the
guineas that were coming slowly through the coming years,
through all his life, which spread far away before him, the end
quite hidden by countless days of weaving.

GEORGE ELIOT, *Silas Marner*

i. What would be a fitting title for this passage?

ii. Make a list of proverbs and sayings connected with
money.

iii. Give alternative words for: monotony, constraint,
revelry, flexibly, earnings, countless. Do you prefer
any of these alternatives to the original words? If so,
why?

iv. Write a description of a spendthrift.

v. Make up a short story of Silas Marner's search for a
lost guinea.

(*k*) We are in a low vaulted room; vaulted, not with arches,
but with small cupolas starred with gold, and chequered with
gloomy figures: in the centre is a bronze font charged with
rich bas-reliefs, a small figure of the Baptist standing above it
in a single ray of light that glances across the narrow room,
dying as it falls from a window high in the wall, and the first
thing that it strikes, and the only thing that it strikes brightly,
is a tomb. We hardly know if it be a tomb indeed; for it is like
a narrow couch set beside the window, low-roofed and cur-
tained, so that it might seem, but that it is some height above

the pavement, to have been drawn towards the window, that the sleeper might be wakened early;—only there are two angels who have drawn the curtain back, and are looking down upon him. Let us look also, and thank that gentle light that rests upon his forehead for ever, and dies away upon his breast.

The face is of a man in middle life, but there are two deep furrows right across the forehead, dividing it like the foundations of a tower: the height of it above is bound by the fillet of the ducal cap. The rest of the features are singularly small and delicate, the lips sharp, perhaps the sharpness of death being added to that of the natural lines; but there is a sweet smile upon them, and a deep serenity upon the whole countenance. The roof of the canopy above has been blue, filled with stars; beneath, in the centre of the tomb on which the figure rests, is a seated figure of the Virgin, and the border of it all around is of flowers and soft leaves, growing rich and deep, as if in a field in summer.

It is the Doge Andrea Dandolo, a man early great among the great of Venice; and early lost. She chose him for her king in his 36th year; he died ten years later, leaving behind him that history to which we owe half of what we know of her former fortunes.

JOHN RUSKIN, *Stones of Venice*

i. Supply a suitable title for the above passage.

ii. Give the meanings of: chequered, bas-relief, ducal, serenity, vaulted, cupola, charged with, font, fillet. Make rough sketches where you can.

iii. Write a short description of any tomb or monument you know.

iv. Describe the features of any bust or statue you have seen.

v. Write down all you know about Venice.

vi. Plan a tour of Italy to last a fortnight in addition to time for travelling there and back. Add a list of things you would particularly like to see during your tour.

VII. COMPOSITION

I. Letters:

    i. To a friend asking for the loan of his bicycle.

    ii. An invitation to a school friend for the summer holidays; describe what he would see and do.

    iii. To a grown-up friend thanking him for a day at the Zoo.

    iv. In acknowledgment of a birthday present.

    v. To a farmer asking his permission to camp on his land. State how long you will be there, how many tents you have, etc.

    vi. To a touring agent asking for cost of a tour you would like to make.

    vii. Three letters written home describing your holidays at different stages.

    viii. To a notable cricketer asking for his autograph.

    ix. A letter of regret that you cannot go to a party. Give reasons why you cannot go.

    x. To a friend asking for the return of a favourite book he has borrowed.

    xi. To a motor firm asking for particulars of a car.

    xii. To a friend inviting him to join you in a river excursion.

    xiii. A letter home describing a day in London, or in some other big town.

    xiv. A letter from school describing the things you enjoy most during the week.

    xv. To your brother who is staying for the holidays with an aunt. Tell him how you spend your time, and how his pets are getting on.

    xvi. To an uncle in reply to a request for a list of books you would like for your birthday of the total value of ten shillings.

xvii. To the editor of your school magazine suggesting improvements.

xviii. To a friend who has asked you to tell him how to make a simple wireless set.

xix. To a railway company about a bag you left in a train; give full particulars.

xx. To a neighbour complaining of his dog.

II. Answering advertisements. Apply for the following situations:

i. Junior clerk required, able to typewrite; letter only, stating age, experience, etc. Messrs John Dorey, 36 Stepgate Street, E.C. 2.

ii. Smart young salesman wanted, age about 18. Write, Webb and Webb, 236 Manchester Street, Liverpool.

iii. Book-keeper, male, wanted, knowledge shorthand essential. Write Box 2376, "Daily Wire."

iv. Intelligent Junior Typist required for London Firm; state experience. Box 263. "Daily Wire."

v. Office Boy (just leaving school) wanted. Prospects for intelligent lad. Borne and Lacy, High Street, E.C. 2.

vi. Laboratory assistant wanted; must have good knowledge of Chemistry up to School Certificate. Maxwell, Chemical Works, Wroxell.

III. Write for further particulars about these advertisements:

i. Bicycle new, unscratched, cost £8, accept reasonable offer. Taylor, 36 Newstead Road, London.

ii. Corona Four Portable Typewriter, brand new, cost £14. 14s. Accept £8. 10s. 8 Mustang Road, S.W. 1.

iii. Pedigree Great Dane, blue, large, massive dog, good guard, 7 guineas; near offer. Particulars, stamp. Winsford, 8 Cranbourne Gardens, Eastbourne.

iv. 1a Folding Kodak, hardly used, with bag, portrait attachment and tripod. Cost £4, sell £2. 15s. Full particulars, Richardson, 62 Walsey Road, Wolverhampton.

v. Student's microscope, 2 objectives, 2 eyepieces, slides. £2. 10s. Apply Turner, 5 Haverfield Road, Sutton.

vi. Dinghy, 12 ft. 6 in. × 4 ft., and Evinnide motor for sale, £15 or separately. Write J. Jordons, 35 Willesdon Avenue, London, E. 1.

vii. 1928 Morris-Cowley 2-seater, maroon, taxed June, perfect condition. What offers? Write Holloway, 7 Luscombe Place, Scarborough.

viii. Collection 400 different stamps, 2s. 9d.; collection 250 different stamps 1s. 6d. Faber, 89 Fairley Road, E.C. 2.

IV. i. You are about to retire, and are looking for a suitable house. Choose the one that attracts you most from these four, and write a letter asking for any further particulars you would like to know.

Convenient Small Country House for sale on edge rural West Kent village: near church, P.O., &c.: charming views all windows: good rooms: three sitting, seven bed, two dressing, one billiard (or box), good kitchen, &c.; central heating, separate hot water; warm garage, good outbuildings; pretty garden, tennis court, short carriage drive, in all about one acre.

Delightful Country Residence, with wooded grounds, overlooking Park; four bed, bath, two reception rooms; large garage; all services; main drainage; station 10 minutes; low price £2300 Freehold. Gerrards Cross.

Devon. A delightful detached sunny Cottage for sale, best part; south aspect; three bed, two sitting, large rooms; gas; main water and drains; matured and charming garden.

Dorset (Blackmoor Vale district). Pre-war Residence, containing 3 reception, 6 bed-rooms, bath-room, usual offices. Garage, small stable and garden. Quiet and convenient position. Price £1300.

    ii. Write a letter to a friend describing the house that you have finally selected.

V. You have won a competition for which the first prize is a £60 pleasure cruise; at least £40 must be spent on shipping fares. The following advertisements have caught your attention. Choose the cruise you would prefer; write a letter to the shipping Company asking for further particulars, and a second letter to a friend explaining why you have made your particular choice.

BLUE STAR LINE

HEALTH & PLEASURE CRUISES
by the World's most Delightful Cruising Liner

"ARANDORA STAR"

Britain's Dream Ship

May 31st .. 17 days from 34 Gns.	To Morocco, Spain, Dalmatia, Italy, Constantinople, Balearic Islands, Atlantic Islands, etc., etc.
June 18th .. 14 days ,, 24 Gns.	
Sept. 19th .. 24 days ,, 48 Gns.	
Oct. 14th .. 24 days ,, 48 Gns.	
July 5th .. 13 days from 20 Gns.	To Norwegian Fjords (Midnight Sun), Northern Capitals, Leningrad for Moscow, etc., etc.
July 19th .. 20 days ,, 30 Gns.	
Aug. 9th .. 13 days ,, 20 Gns.	
Aug. 23rd .. 23 days ,, 40 Gns.	

Spacious decks, delightful ballroom, restful sun deck away from games. Swimming pool. Louis XIV restaurant, with exceptional cuisine and service, accommodating all passengers at one sitting.

Tastefully appointed state rooms throughout, with bedsteads and hot and cold running water. Luxurious public rooms on a scale obtainable only on the

"ARANDORA STAR"

Early bookings secure preference in accommodation.

For South American and Eastern sailings, also "Arandora Star" Cruise Programme apply Blue Star Line, 3 Lower Regent-street ('Phone, Gerrard 5671).

HOLIDAYS ON THE SEA

Pleasant Summer Ocean Trips at Reduced Rates. A Month on the Sea (14 days either way) and a week's Motor Tour through Beautiful Jamaica. £60.

Five weeks Round Voyage to West Indies and Spanish Main. £50.
First Class Only

Regular Passenger Services to Jamaica, Barbados, Trinidad, Panama, Costa Rica, Colombia, Honduras. Through bookings to Pacific Ports of Central, North, and South America.

For full particulars apply to:

Elders and Fyffes, Limited, 31 Bow-street, W.C. 2, Temple Bar 5555.

VI. Telegrams.

   i. To a friend giving time of arrival on a visit.

   ii. To a London firm saying that the goods you ordered have not come; they are urgently needed. Write their telegraphed reply as well.

  iii. Instructions to a friend as to train and meeting-place. You are going off for a day's walking and have agreed to meet at 9 o'clock in the morning.

  iv. To a cricket team cancelling a match on account of rain.

   v. Ordering a taxi to meet you at a station.

  vi. Regretting inability to attend a birthday party. You have caught a cold.

 vii. For a spare part for a bicycle.

viii. Cancelling a berth on a liner.

  ix. Booking a seat at a concert.

   x. To a friend, from a village where your car has broken down.

VII. Questions to answer.

    i. How is a wasp's nest constructed?
    ii. What causes the tides?
    iii. How are the seasons caused?
    iv. How has coal been formed?
    v. How is lime made?
    vi. What is brass?
    vii. How do you print a photograph from the negative?
    viii. How is a ship steered?
    ix. How are bricks made?
    x. How does a padlock work?
    xi. How does a miner's safety-lamp work?
    xii. How is cane sugar made?
    xiii. How is a glass tumbler made?
    xiv. Why are flies dangerous?
    xv. How does a plant grow?
    xvi. How does a canal-lock work?
    xvii. How does the telephone work?
    xviii. How does a fire-engine work?
    xix. What are railway points for?
    xx. How is a rocket apparatus worked?
    xxi. How is a carpet made?
    xxii. How is a vase made?
    xxiii. How is a candle made?
    xxiv. How does a barometer work?
    xxv. How do birds help the farmer?

VIII. State what you know of the work of

    i. A farm labourer.
    ii. A coal miner.
    iii. A policeman.
    iv. An engine driver.

     v. A dustman.

    vi. A bishop.

   vii. A magistrate.

  viii. A chauffeur.

    ix. A chimney sweeper.

     x. A bus driver.

    xi. A bank cashier.

   xii. A museum curator.

  xiii. A builder.

  xiv. An architect.

   xv. A town councillor.

  xvi. An electrical engineer.

 xvii. An astronomer.

xviii. A schoolmaster.

  xix. A gardener.

   xx. A butcher.

IX. Autobiographies of

     i. Yourself.

    ii. Your school cap.

   iii. A pound note.

   iv. A bottle washed up on the sea shore.

    v. An eel.

   vi. A tent.

  vii. Your boots.

 viii. A railway engine.

   ix. A letter from France.

    x. A tin of salmon.

   xi. Your school desk.

  xii. A thrush.

  xiii. A rose.

  xiv. A shaving brush.

xv. A lawn mower.
xvi. A tramp.
xvii. A buccaneer.
xviii. An arctic explorer.
xix. A knight of King Arthur.
xx. A doctor.

X. Extracts from the diaries of

i. A marooned pirate.
ii. A Pekinese dog.
iii. A London policeman.
iv. A fireman.
v. A railway signalman.
vi. A motor bicycle.
vii. A schoolmaster.
viii. A sign post at the cross roads.
ix. A Norman castle.
x. A schoolboy.
xi. A Roman road.
xii. A bank clerk.
xiii. An African explorer.
xiv. A mountaineer.
xv. An airman.
xvi. A deep-sea fisherman.
xvii. A boy scout.
xviii. An exhibit in a museum.
xix. An oak tree.
xx. An Elizabethan seaman.

XI. Things to describe.

i. A table laid for breakfast.
ii. A hearthrug.
iii. An electric-light bulb.
iv. The front of your home.

v. The outside of the Town Hall.

vi. The inside of the Town Hall.

vii. The main street of your town.

viii. A shop window and its contents.

ix. An advertisement hoarding.

x. A fountain pen.

xi. A camera.

xii. The most comfortable chair you know.

xiii. A cycle lamp.

xiv. A step-ladder.

xv. A lawn mower.

xvi. A bath chair.

xvii. A typewriter.

xviii. An omnibus.

xix. A steam roller.

xx. A penknife.

XII. People to describe.

i. Another boy (or girl) in your form.

ii. The Prime Minister.

iii. A famous tennis player.

iv. A popular cricketer.

v. The mayor of your town.

vi. The Prince of Wales.

vii. Your father.

viii. The captain of the school.

ix. A well-known author.

x. Any famous historical character.

xi. A character from fiction.

xii. The Archbishop of Canterbury.

xiii. The school porter.

xiv. Your ideal king.

xv. The captain of the English XI.

xvi. A pirate.
xvii. Your doctor.
xviii. A great explorer.
xix. The postman.
xx. A great scientist.

XIII. Stories to be continued.

i. The two boys were hurrying through Hoppitt's Wood on their way home after a day's rambling, when suddenly...

ii. Of the three men in the railway carriage, two were old friends and the third a stranger to them. He was deeply interested in his newspaper. One of the friends said to the other, "You see if I don't manage somehow to make him put down that newspaper"....

iii. A tall man was standing in front of a case in the British Museum. To any passer-by he seemed intent on studying the flint arrow-heads that were displayed. Presently he looked round as if to see if the gallery were empty, and...

iv. Just as the train was starting, a man rushed from the Booking Office and jumped into a first-class compartment in which an elderly gentleman was reading a magazine. A quarter of an hour later, the train came to a sudden stop, as the communication chain had been pulled...

v. The cross-channel steamer was crowded, and many were the complaints made at the lack of accommodation. One man told the steward that while he was in the saloon, his...

vi. "Can you give me a clear account of what happened?" asked the police inspector.
"Well, it was like this. I was driving quite slowly, when..."

vii. The angler had spent a pleasant and successful day, but his hope of a quiet evening by the inn fire was not to be fulfilled...

viii. "You see that lion?" said the keeper.
"Yes, what about him?" asked the visitor.
"There's a queer story told about him. When he arrived here..."

ix. Mr Cripps was feeling rather tired. He had been walking all day over the Downs in the hot sunshine, and was now plodding along the main road back to the station. For some time he noticed two figures coming towards him; as they drew level with him, they...

x. The excitement was intense. Nettlefield had made 112 in their innings, and now Tolsley were batting. The last man was in, and the score was 110...

XIV. Write short stories to illustrate the following proverbs:

i. A bird in the hand is worth two in the bush.

ii. A stitch in time saves nine.

iii. Where there's a will there's a way.

iv. Better an empty house than an ill tenant.

v. Penny wise and pound foolish.

vi. "He that is soon angry will deal foolishly."
(*Proverbs* XIV, 17.)

vii. "A soft answer turneth away wrath."
(*Proverbs* XV, 1.)

viii. "Better is a little with righteousness
Than great revenues with injustice." (*Proverbs* XVI, 8.)

ix. "The borrower is servant to the lender."
(*Proverbs* XXII, 7.)

x. "The forcing of wrath bringeth forth strife."
(*Proverbs* XXX, 33.)

xi. All is not gold that glitters.

xii. More haste less speed.

xiii. Onlookers see most of the game.

xiv. Absence makes the heart grow fonder.

xv. Out of sight, out of mind.

XV. Write anecdotes to bring out the meanings of the following sayings:

    i. His bark is worse than his bite.
    ii. In leading strings.
    iii. In the same boat.
    iv. The worst come to the worst.
    v. No love lost between.
    vi. Coming events cast their shadow before.
    vii. Against the grain.
    viii. The bubble burst.

XVI. Give clear directions for doing the following:

    i. Buying a railway ticket.
    ii. Marking out a cricket pitch.
    iii. Erecting a tent.
    iv. Starting a stamp collection.
    v. Sending a telegram.
    vi. Calling up on the telephone.
    vii. Copying a map.
    viii. Wrapping up a parcel.
    ix. Frying bacon.
    x. Making a model aeroplane.
    xi. Making toast.
    xii. Cleaning boots.
    xiii. Filling a fountain pen.
    xiv. Addressing an envelope.
    xv. Registering a letter.
    xvi. Mending a puncture.
    xvii. Attending to a cut finger.
    xviii. Making hydrogen.
    xix. Fitting up an electric bell.
    xx. Putting a paper cover on a book.

XVII. Dialogues between

    i. An airman and a pedestrian.
    ii. Queen Elizabeth and Queen Victoria.
    iii. An English schoolboy and a French schoolboy.
    iv. The captain of a tramp steamer and the captain of an ocean liner.
    v. David Livingstone and Captain Scott.
    vi. A cricketer and a footballer.
    vii. An author and an explorer.
    viii. A photographer and a portrait painter.
    ix. A shopkeeper and a farmer.
    x. A member of Parliament and a voter.
    xi. A fishing smack and a yacht.
    xii. An ancient Briton and a modern man.
    xiii. A steeple-jack and a coal miner.
    xiv. Two characters from two different novels.
    xv. Sherlock Holmes and Doctor Watson.
    xvi. Julius Caesar and William the Conqueror.
    xvii. Marconi and Edison.
    xviii. A Ford car and a Rolls Royce.
    xix. The President of France and the President of the U.S.A.
    xx. The editor of *The Times* and the editor of your school magazine.

XVIII. Write out notes for speeches on the following subjects. Choose the point of view you favour:

    i. That braces are better than belts.
    ii. That ghosts do not exist.
    iii. That a speed limit is desirable for motor cars.
    iv. That everyone should have a hobby.
    v. That there should be more practical work in school.

vi. That life in the Middle Ages was more exciting than present-day life.

vii. That "Safety First" is a selfish policy.

viii. That "Handsome is as handsome does".

ix. That homework is necessary.

x. That Rugger is a better team game than Soccer.

xi. That our towns are getting too large.

xii. That motoring has spoilt the countryside.

xiii. That all men are equal.

xiv. That prizes should not be awarded in schools.

xv. That the League of Nations promotes good feeling among the different peoples.

xvi. That detective novels exaggerate the cleverness of criminals.

xvii. That all railways should be electrified.

xviii. That cigarette smoking is a silly habit.

xix. That shorts are preferable to trousers.

xx. That Napoleon did more harm than good.

XIX. Write accounts of the following events in any form you like, e.g. letter, dramatic scene, narrative, etc.:

i. William the Conqueror lands in England, 1066.

ii. King John signs Magna Carta, 1215.

iii. John Ball preaches to the peasants, 1381.

iv. Caxton prints his first book in England, 1477.

v. John Cabot receives letters-patent from Henry VII to sail on a voyage from Bristol, 1496.

vi. Luther appears before Charles V at Worms, 1521.

vii. Queen Elizabeth visits Francis Drake on board *The Golden Hind*, 1579.

viii. Cromwell dismisses the Rump Parliament, 1653.

ix. James II secretly takes flight from England, 1688.

x. The Young Pretender lands in Scotland, 1745.

xi. Edmund Burke in the House of Commons supports the American Colonies, 1774.

xii. Sir William Herschel discovers the planet Uranus, 1781.

xiii. At a martello tower on the south coast of England, 1804.

xiv. The first run on the Stockton-Darlington Railway, 1825.

xv. The passing of the Reform Bill, 1832, in the House of Commons.

xvi. The arrival of the first trans-Atlantic steamships, *Sirius* and *Great Western*, at New York, 1838.

xvii. Florence Nightingale in the Crimean hospitals, 1854.

xviii. The assassination of Abraham Lincoln, 1865.

xix. Marconi's first wireless message across the Channel, 1899.

xx. The arrival at Clifden (Ireland) of Alcock and Brown in the first one-flight air crossing of the Atlantic, 1919.

XX. "If" situations to consider and write about.

i. If Harold had won the Battle of Hastings...

ii. If gunpowder had not been invented...

iii. If all the books of Euclid had been lost...

iv. If the Young Pretender had captured London in 1745...

v. If thoughts were visible...

vi. If dogs could talk...

vii. If the Channel dried up...

viii. If all bird-life became extinct...

ix. If television becomes practicable for everyone...

x. If the sun lost its heat...

XXI. General subjects for writing.

1. Railway posters.
2. Common-sense.
3. The House of Commons.
4. Bridges.
5. Sherlock Holmes.
6. Roman roads.
7. A parish church.
8. Farming.
9. Newspapers.
10. An English Prime Minister.
11. The ideal labour-saving house.
12. A clever invention.
13. Bees.
14. Our weather.
15. The Border Land.
16. Castles.
17. The best game for boys (or girls).
18. Winter sports.
19. London.
20. A famous inn.
21. A character from Dickens.
22. Clocks.
23. A park and its trees.
24. Footpaths.
25. Crossing the channel.
26. The latest type of railway locomotive.
27. My county.
28. Chemistry in ordinary life.
29. Common uses of electricity.
30. Gilbert and Sullivan.
31. The camera.
32. Camp life.
33. The Stuarts.
34. The clipper ships.
35. Sea shanties.
36. Folk dancing.
37. A European capital.
38. Growing up.
39. Trackways of England.
40. Canals.
41. Learning to swim.
42. Kipling's *Kim*.
43. When knights were bold.
44. The Rhine.
45. Amateur acting.
46. Lawn tennis.
47. Exploration in Africa.
48. The Pilgrim's Way.
49. Conjuring.
50. Poultry keeping.
51. The Ordnance Survey maps.
52. Gymnastics.
53. Pedestrian and motorist.
54. Mountain scenery.
55. Fireworks.
56. Lifeboats.
57. The Argonauts.
58. Carpentry as a hobby.
59. A small garden.
60. War memorials.
61. The Great North Road.

62. Lighthouses.
63. The Elizabethan theatre.
64. The gamekeeper.
65. Handwriting.
66. The making of glass.
67. Heraldry.
68. Hunting with a camera.
69. Freshwater fishing.
70. Village life.
71. Postage stamps.
72. Chess.
73. My dog.
74. Peter Pan.
75. Animals' rights.
76. The moon.
77. The small allotment garden.
78. Toy making.
79. Crystal receiving sets.
80. Sketching in pencil.
81. Tulips.
82. A walking tour.
83. Broadcasting.
84. Making bread.
85. Familiar quotations from Shakespeare.
86. The Roman Empire.
87. The Jacobites.
88. The chemistry of chalk.
89. Pond life.
90. A great inventor.
91. Road making.
92. The hedgerow.
93. A great physician.
94. Our town council.
95. Fox terriers.
96. The Isle of Man.
97. The Census.
98. Domestic animals.
99. Our coinage.
100. Ballads of Robin Hood.

VIII. VERSE

I. Supply the missing rimes for the following lines. The rime scheme is indicated by letters:

(a) What's become of Waring   a
    Since he gave us all the ——,   b
    Chose land-travel or ——,   a
    Boots and chest or staff and scrip,   b
    Rather than pace up and down   c
    Any longer London ——?   c
    Who'd have guessed it from his ——   b
    Or his brow's accustomed ——,   a
    On the night he thus took ——,   b
    Or started landward?—little ——   a
    For us, it seems, who supped ——   d
    (Friends of his too, I remember)   e
    And walked home through the merry weather,   d
    The snowiest in all ——.   e
    I left his arm that night ——   f
    For what's-his-name's, the new prose-poet   g
    That wrote the book there, on the shelf—   f
    How, forsooth, was I to ——   g
    If Waring meant to glide ——   h
    Like a ghost at break of day?   h
    Never looked he half so ——!   h

                           ROBERT BROWNING, *Waring*

(b) I know a Mount, the gracious Sun perceives   a
    First when he visits, last, too, when he ——   a
    The world; and, vainly favoured, it ——   b
    The day-long glory of his steadfast gaze   b
    By no change of its large calm front of ——.   c
    And underneath the Mount, a Flower I know,   c
    He cannot have perceived, that changes ——   d
    At his approach; and, in the lost endeavour   d
    To live his life, has parted, one by ——,   e
    With all a flower's true graces, for the ——   f
    Of being but a foolish mimic sun,   e
    With ray-like florets round a disk-like face.   f

Men nobly call by many a name the Mount   g
As over many a land of theirs its ——   h
Calm front of snow like a triumphal targe   h
Is reared, and still with old names, fresh ones ——, i
Each to its proper praise and own ——:   g
Men call the Flower, the Sunflower, sportively. i

ROBERT BROWNING, *Rudel to the Lady of Tripoli*

(*c*) I hate that drum's discordant sound,   a
    Parading round, and round, and ——:   a
    To thoughtless youth it pleasure ——,   b
    And lures from cities and from fields,   b
    To sell their liberty for ——   c
    Of tawdry lace, and glittering arms;   c
    And when ambition's voice commands,   d
    To march, and fight, and fall, in foreign ——.   d

J. SCOTT, *Ode on Hearing the Drum*

(*d*) There stands a City,—neither large nor small,—   a
    Its air and situation sweet and ——;   b
It matters very little—if at —— —   a
    Whether its denizens are dull or witty, b
Whether the ladies there are short or ——,   a
    Brunettes or blondes, only, there stands a ——!——   b
Perhaps 'tis also requisite to ——   c
That there's a Castle and a Cobbler in it.   c

R. H. BARHAM ("INGOLDSBY"), *The Ghost*

(*e*) Victorious men of earth, no ——   a
    Proclaim how wide your empires are;   b
Though you bind in every shore,   a
    And your triumphs reach as ——   b
      As night or day,   c
    Yet you, proud monarchs, must ——   c
And mingle with forgotten ashes, ——   d
Death calls ye to the crowd of common men.   d

Devouring Famine, Plague, and War,   e
    Each able to undo ——,   f
Death's servile emissaries ——;   e
    Nor to these alone confined,   f

He hath at ——   g
  More quaint and subtle ways to kill;   g
A smile or kiss, as he will use the ——,   h
Shall have the cunning skill to break a heart.   h

J. SHIRLEY, Victorious Men

(*f*) How like the leper, with his own sad ——   a
  Enforcing his own solitude, it tolls!   b
  That lonely bell set in the rushing ——,   b
  To warn us from the place of jeopardy!   a
  O friend of man! sore-vexed by ocean's ——,   c
  The changing tides wash o'er thee day by —— ;   d
  Thy trembling mouth is filled with bitter spray,   d
  Yet still thou ringest on from hour to hour;   c
  High is thy mission, though thy lot is —— —   e
  To be in danger's realm a guardian —— ;   f
  In seamen's dreams a pleasant part to bear,   g
  And earn their blessing as the year goes round;   f
  And strike the key-note of each grateful ——,   g
  Breathed in their distant homes by wife or child!   e

C. TENNYSON TURNER, The Buoy Bell

(*g*) In Christian world Mary the garland —— !   a
  Rebecca sweetens on a Hebrew's ear;   b
  Quakers for pure Priscilla are more —— ;   b
  And the light Gaul by amorous Ninon swears.   a
  Among the lesser lights how Lucy —— !   c
  What air of fragrance Rosamond throws around!   d
  How like a hymn doth sweet Cecilia —— !   d
  Of Marthas, and of Abigails, few lines   c
  Have bragged in verse. Of coarsest household stuff e
  Should homely Joan be fashionèd. But ——   f
  You Barbara resist, or Marian?   f
  And is not Clare for love excuse —— ?   e
  Yet, by my faith in numbers, I ——,   g
  These all, than Saxon Edith, please me less.   g

C. LAMB, Sonnet on Christian Names

II. Divide the following passages into lines of blank
  verse:

(*a*) Books are not seldom talismans and spells, by which the
magic art of shrewder wits holds an unthinking multitude
enthralled. Some to the fascination of a name surrender judgement, hoodwinked. Some the style infatuates, and through
labyrinths and wilds of error leads them by a tune entranced.
While sloth seduces more, too weak to bear the insupportable
fatigue of thought, and swallowing, therefore, without pause
or choice, the total grist unsifted, husks and all.

W. COWPER, The Task

(*b*) Forth I sail'd into the deep illimitable main, with but one
bark, and the small faithful band that yet cleaved to me. As
Iberia far, far as Marocco, either shore I saw, and the Sardinian
and each isle beside which round that ocean bathes. Tardy with
age were I and my companions, when we came to the strait
pass, where Hercules ordain'd the boundaries not to be
o'erstepped by man. The walls of Seville to my right I left, on
the other hand already Ceuta past.

H. CARY's translation of DANTE's Inferno

(*c*) Faint not in the moment of victory! our ends, and
Warwick's head, innocent Warwick's head (for we are prologue
but to his tragedy), conclude the wonder of Henry's fears: and
then the glorious race of fourteen kings Plantagenets, deter-
mines in this last issue male. Heaven be obeyed. Impoverish
time of its amazement, friends; and we will prove as trusty in
our payments, as prodigal to nature in our debts.

JOHN FORD, Perkin Warbeck

(*d*) The trees which grew along the broken arches waved
dark in the blue midnight, and the stars shone through the
rents of ruin; from afar the watch-dog bay'd beyond the Tiber;
and more near from out the Cæsars' palace came the owl's
long cry, and, interruptedly, of distant sentinels the fitful song
begun and died upon the gentle wind. Some cypresses beyond
the time-worn breach appear'd to skirt the horizon, yet they
stood within a bowshot.

LORD BYRON, Manfred

(*e*) No forest fell when thou wouldst build, no quarry sent its stores to enrich thy walls; but thou didst hew the floods, and make thy marble of the glassy wave. In such a palace Aristæus found Cyrene, when he bore the plaintive tale of his lost bees to her maternal ear: in such a palace Poetry might place the armoury of Winter; where his troops, the gloomy clouds, find weapons, arrowy sleet, skin-piercing volley, blossom-bruising hail, and snow that often blinds the traveller's course, and wraps him in an unexpected tomb. Silently as a dream the fabric rose; no sound of hammer or of saw was there. Ice upon ice, the well-adjusted parts were soon conjoined, nor other cement asked than water interfused to make them one.

W. Cowper, *The Task*

(*f*) The forest deer, being struck, runs to an herb that closeth up the wounds: but when the imperial lion's flesh is gor'd, he rends and tears it with his wrathful paw, (and,) highly scorning that the lowly earth should drink his blood, mounts up to the air: and so it fares with me, whose dauntless mind th' ambitious Mortimer would seek to curb, and that unnatural queen, false Isabel, that thus hath pent and mew'd me in a prison; for such outrageous passions cloy my soul, as with the wings of rancour and disdain full oft(en) am I soaring up to heaven, to plain me to the gods against them both.

C. Marlowe, *Edward II*

III. Comment on the effectiveness and suitability of the similes and metaphors in the following passages. Suggest other similes for the same subjects.

(*a*)
> Courage, my soul! now learn to wield
> The weight of thine immortal shield;
> Close on thy head thy helmet bright;
> Balance thy sword against the fight;
> See where an army, strong as fair,
> With silken banners spreads the air!

Andrew Marvell, *A Dialogue*

(*b*)
> The Assyrian came down like the wolf on the fold,
> And his cohorts were gleaming in purple and gold;
> And the sheen of their spears was like stars on the sea,
> When the blue wave rolls nightly on deep Galilee.

Like the leaves of the forest when Summer is green,
That host with their banners at sunset were seen:
Like the leaves of the forest when Autumn hath blown,
That host on the morrow lay withered and strown.

LORD BYRON, *The Destruction of Sennacherib*

(*c*)   Day after day, day after day,
             We stuck, nor breath nor motion;
             As idle as a painted ship
             Upon a painted ocean.

S. T. COLERIDGE, *The Ancient Mariner*

(*d*)   Life's a name
         That nothing here can truly claim;
     This wretched inn, where we scarce stay to bait,
         We call our dwelling-place!

A. COWLEY, *Life*

(*e*) Here stood a shatter'd archway plumed with fern;
     And here had fall'n a great part of a tower,
     Whole, like a crag that tumbles from the cliff,
     And like a crag was gay with wilding flowers.

LORD TENNYSON, *The Marriage of Geraint*

(*f*) Hail, adamantine Steel! magnetic Lord!
     King of the prow, the ploughshare, and the sword!
     True to the pole, by thee the pilot guides
     His steady helm amid the struggling tides;
     Braves with broad sail the immeasurable sea,
     Cleaves the dark air, and asks no star but thee.—
     By thee the ploughshare rends the matted plain,
     Inhumes in level rows the living grain;
     Intrusive forests quit the cultured ground,
     And Ceres laughs, with golden fillets crowned.—
     O'er restless realms, when scowling discord flings
     Her snakes, and loud the din of battle rings;
     Expiring strength, and vanquished courage feel
     Thy arm resistless, adamantine Steel!

E. DARWIN, *Steel*

(g) Like to the falling of a star,
Or as the flights of eagles are,—
Or like the fresh spring's gaudy hue,
Or silver drops of morning dew;
Or like a wind that chafes the flood,
Or bubbles which on water stood:
Even such is man, whose borrowed light
Is straight called in, and paid to night.
The wind blows out, the bubble dies;
The spring entombed in autumn lies;
The dew dries up, the star is shot;
The flight is past—and man forgot.

H. KING, *Sic Vita*

(h) All round the coast the languid air did swoon,
Breathing like one that hath a weary dream.
Full-faced above the valley stood the moon;
And like a downward smoke, the slender stream
Along the cliff to fall and pause and fall did seem.

LORD TENNYSON, *The Lotos-Eaters*

(i) And the leaves, brown, yellow, and gray, and red,
And white with the whiteness of what is dead,
Like troops of ghosts on the dry wind passed;
Their whistling noise made the birds aghast.

P. B. SHELLEY, *The Sensitive Plant*

(j) As the wolves, that headlong go
On the stately buffalo,
Though with fiery eyes, and angry roar,
And hoofs that stamp, and horns that gore,
He tramples on earth, or tosses on high
The foremost, who rush on his strength but to die:
Thus against the wall they went,
Thus the first were backward bent;
Many a bosom, sheathed in brass,
Strew'd the earth like broken glass,
Shiver'd by the shot, that tore
The ground whereon they moved no more:
Even as they fell, in files they lay,
Like the mower's grass at the close of day,

When his work is done on the levell'd plain;
Such was the fall of the foremost slain.

LORD BYRON, *The Siege of Corinth*

(*k*)   Hark! the cock crows, and yon bright star
           Tells us the day himself's not far;
           And see where, breaking from the night,
           He gilds the western hills with light.
           With him old Janus doth appear,
           Peeping into the future year,
           With such a look as seems to say,
           The prospect is not good that way.

CHARLES COTTON, *The New Year*

(*l*)   Then fly our greetings, fly our speech and smiles!
              —As some grave Tyrian trader, from the sea,
              Descried at sunrise an emerging prow
           Lifting the cool-hair'd creepers stealthily,
              The fringes of a southward-facing brow
                 Among the Ægean isles;
           And saw the merry Grecian coaster come,
              Freighted with amber grapes, and Chian wine,
              Green, bursting figs, and tunnies steep'd in brine;
           And knew the intruders on his ancient home,

           The young light-hearted masters of the waves;
              And snatch'd his rudder, and shook out more sail,
                 And day and night held on indignantly
           O'er the blue Midland waters with the gale,
                 Betwixt the Syrtes and soft Sicily,
                    To where the Atlantic raves
           Outside the western straits, and unbent sails
                 There where down cloudy cliffs, through sheets of
                 foam,
              Shy traffickers, the dark Iberians come;
           And on the beach undid his corded bales.

M. ARNOLD, *The Scholar-Gipsy*

IV. Exercises on the passages that follow.

  i. Scan the lines.

 ii. Point out any lines or passages that particularly please
     you, and try to find out the reason for your pleasure.

iii. Comment on the figures of speech.

iv. Describe the scenes suggested.

v. What effect has each passage on you?

vi. Discuss the suitability of the metres to the themes.

vii. Write verses of your own in the various metres on any subjects you think suitable.

(a)
    The castled crag of Drachenfels
    Frowns o'er the wide and winding Rhine,
    Whose breast of waters broadly swells
    Between the banks which bear the vine,
    And hills all rich with blossomed trees,
    And fields which promise corn and wine,
    And scattered cities crowning these,
    Whose far white walls along them shine,
    Have strewed a scene, which I should see
    With double joy wert *thou* with me.

LORD BYRON, *Childe Harold's Pilgrimage*

(b)
    Oh, to be in England
    Now that April's there,
    And whoever wakes in England
    Sees, some morning, unaware,
    That the lowest boughs and the brushwood sheaf
    Round the elm-tree bole are in tiny leaf,
    While the chaffinch sings on the orchard bough
    In England—now!

ROBERT BROWNING, *Home-Thoughts, from Abroad*

(c)
    But who the melodies of morn can tell—
    The wild brook babbling down the mountain side;
    The lowing herd, the sheepfold's simple bell;
    The pipe of early shepherd dim descried
    In the lone valley; echoing far and wide
    The clamorous horn along the cliffs above;
    The hollow murmur of the ocean-tide;
    The hum of bees, the linnet's lay of love,
  And the full choir that wakes the universal grove?

J. BEATTIE, *The Minstrel*

(*d*) The squirrel gloats on his accomplished hoard,
The ants have brimmed their garners with ripe grain,
    And honey bees have stored
The sweets of Summer in their luscious cells;
The swallows all have winged across the main;
But here the Autumn melancholy dwells,
    And sighs her tearful spells
Amongst the sunless shadows of the plain.

                                  T. Hood, *Ode: Autumn*

(*e*)   Dark, deep, and cold the current flows
      Unto the sea where no wind blows,
      Seeking the land which no one knows.
      O'er its sad gloom still comes and goes
      The mingled wail of friends and foes,
      Borne to the land which no one knows.

                         E. Elliott, *The Land which no one knows*

(*f*)   The old house stooped just like a cave,
         Thatched o'er with mosses green;
      Winter around the walls would rave,
         But all was calm within;
      The trees are here all green agen,
         Here bees the flowers still kiss,
      But flowers and trees seemed sweeter then:
         My early home was this.

                           J. Clare, *My Early Home*

(*g*) A mist was driving down the British Channel,
      The day was just begun,
And through the window-panes, on floor and panel,
      Streamed the red autumn sun.

It glanced on flowing flag and rippling pennon,
      And the white sails of ships;
And, from the frowning rampart, the black cannon
      Hailed it with feverish lips.

          H. W. Longfellow, *The Warden of The Cinque Ports*

(*h*)   He did not strike one blow,
         For the recreants came behind,
      In a place where the hornbeams grow,
         A path right hard to find,
      For the hornbeam boughs swing so,
         That the twilight makes it blind.

                  William Morris, *Shameful Death*

(i)   We are the music-makers,
          And we are the dreamers of dreams,
        Wandering by lone sea-breakers,
          And sitting by desolate streams;
        World-losers and world-forsakers,
          On whom the pale moon gleams:
        Yet we are the movers and shakers
          Of the world for ever, it seems.

                              A. W. E. O'Shaughnessy, *Ode*

(j)   For the tender beech and the sapling oak,
          That grow by the shadowy rill,
        You may cut down both at a single stroke,
          You may cut down which you will.
        But this you must know, that as long as they grow,
          Whatsoever change may be,
        You can never teach either oak or beech
          To be aught but a greenwood tree.

                              T. L. Peacock, *Maid Marian*

(k)   Behold the market-place with poor o'erspread!
        The Man of Ross divides the weekly bread;
        He feeds yon almshouse, neat, but void of state,
        Where Age and Want sit smiling at the gate;
        Him portioned maids, apprenticed orphans blessed,
        The young who labour, and the old who rest.
        Is any sick? the Man of Ross relieves,
        Prescribes, attends, the medicine makes, and gives.
        Is there a variance? enter but his door,
        Balked are the courts, and contest is no more.
        Despairing quacks with curses fled the place,
        And vile attorneys, now a useless race.

                              A. Pope, *The Man of Ross*

(l)   Sleep, Mr Speaker; it's surely fair
        If you don't in your bed, that you should in your chair.
        Longer and longer still they grow,
        Tory and Radical, Aye and No;
        Talking by night, and talking by day;—
        Sleep, Mr Speaker; sleep, sleep while you may!

                              W. M. Praed, *Stanzas to the Speaker Asleep*

(*m*)   A gentle knight was pricking on the plain,
      Yclad in mighty arms and silver shield,
      Wherein old dints of deep wounds did remain,
      The cruel marks of many a bloody field;
      Yet arms till that time did he never wield.
      His angry steed did chide his foaming bit,
      As much disdaining to the curb to yield:
      Full jolly knight he seemed and fair did sit,
   As one for knightly jousts and fierce encounters fit.

                      E. SPENSER, *Faerie Queene*

(*n*)   The splendour falls on castle walls
         And snowy summits old in story:
      The long light shakes across the lakes,
         And the wild cataract leaps in glory.
    Blow, bugle, blow, set the wild echoes flying,
    Blow, bugle; answer, echoes, dying, dying, dying.

                      LORD TENNYSON, *The Princess*

(*o*)   A pleasing land of drowsyhed it was:
      Of dreams that wave before the half-shut eye;
      And of gay castles in the clouds that pass,
      For ever flushing round a summer sky:
      There eke the soft delights that witchingly
      Instil a wanton sweetness through the breast,
      And the calm pleasures always hovered nigh;
      But whate'er smacked of noyance, or unrest,
  Was far far off expelled from this delicious nest.

             J. THOMSON, *The Castle of Indolence*

(*p*)   I walked the other day—to spend my hour—
        Into a field,
      Where I sometimes had seen the soil to yield
        A gallant flower,
      But Winter now had ruffled all the bower,
        And curious store
      I knew there heretofore.

                      W. VAUGHAN

(*q*) I think I could turn and live with animals, they are so
      placid and self-contained;
   I stand and look at them long and long.

They do not sweat and whine about their condition;
They do not lie awake in the dark and weep for their sins;
They do not make me sick discussing their duty to God;
Not one is dissatisfied—not one is demented with the mania of
    owning things;
Not one kneels to another, nor to his kind that lived thousands
    of years ago;
Not one is respectable or industrious over the whole earth.

WALT WHITMAN, *Song of Myself*

(*r*) It is not to be thought of that the flood
     Of British freedom, which, to the open sea
     Of the world's praise, from dark antiquity
     Hath flowed, "with pomp of waters, unwithstood",
     Roused though it be full often to a mood
     Which spurns the check of salutary bands,
     That this most famous Stream in bogs and sands
     Should perish; and to evil and to good
     Be lost for ever. In our halls is hung
     Armoury of the invincible knights of old:
     We must be free or die, who speak the tongue
     That Shakespeare spoke; the faith and morals hold
     Which Milton held.—In everything we are sprung
     Of Earth's first blood, have titles manifold.

W. WORDSWORTH

(*s*) There is a desert of dread in the uttermost part of the world,
     Where over a wall of mountains is a mighty water hurled,
     Whose hidden head none knoweth, nor where it meeteth
       the sea;
     And that force is the Force of Andvari, and an Elf of the
       Dark is he.
     In the cloud and the desert he dwelleth amid that land
       alone;
     And his work is the storing of treasure within his house
       of stone.

WILLIAM MORRIS, *Sigurd*

(*t*)   Seventeen hundred and thirty-nine:—
          That was the date of this tale of mine.

          First great George was buried and gone;
          George the Second was plodding on.

London then, as the "Guides" aver,
Shared its glories with *Westminster*.
And people of rank, to correct their "tone,"
Went out of town to *Marybone*.

AUSTIN DOBSON, *Ballad of " Beau Brocade"*

(*u*)   The first strong dore that they cam at,
  They loosed it without a key;
The next chaind dore that they cam at,
  They gard it a' in flinders flee.

(*Ballad*)

(*v*)   He has gotten a coat of the even cloth,
  And a pair of shoes of velvet green,
And till seven years were past and gone
  True Thomas on earth was never seen.

(*Ballad*)

(*w*)   Broad-browed he was, hook-nosed, with wide grey eyes
No longer eager for the coming prize,
But keen and steadfast, many an ageing line,
Half hidden by his sweeping beard and fine,
Ploughed his thin cheeks, his hair was more than grey,
And like to one he seemed whose better day
Is over to himself, though foolish fame
Shouts louder year by year his empty name.
Unarmed he was, nor clad upon that morn
Much like a king, an ivory hunting-horn
Was slung about him, rich with gems and gold,
And a great white ger-falcon did he hold
Upon his fist.

WILLIAM MORRIS, *Earthly Paradise* (Prologue)

(*x*)   For out from countless coverts, from low palm-shaded
  islands,
  That fledged in seeming innocence the smooth and
  shining main,
The pinnaces came gliding and hemmed them round in
  silence,
  All manned with Indian bravos and whiskered dogs
  of Spain.

EDMUND JONES, *The Cruise of the Rover*

(*y*) The moon came white and ghostly as we laid the treasure
down,
There was gear there'd make a beggarman as rich as
Lima Town,
Copper charms and silver trinkets from the chests of
Spanish crews,
Gold doubloons and double moidores, louis d'ors and
portagues,
Clumsy yellow-metal earrings from the Indians of Brazil,
Uncut emeralds out of Rio, bezoar stones from Guayaquil;
Silver, in the crude and fashioned, pots of old Arica
bronze,
Jewels from the bones of Incas desecrated by the Dons.

JOHN MASEFIELD, *Spanish Waters*

(*z*) But Jason, going swiftly with good heart
Came to the wished-for shrine built all apart
Midmost the temple, that on pillars stood
Of jasper green, and marble red as blood,
All white itself and carven cunningly
With Neptune bringing from the wavy sea
The golden shining ram to Athamas.

WILLIAM MORRIS, *Life and Death of Jason*

(*aa*) Stiff flags straining in the night-blasts cold
In the gloom black-purple, in the glint old-gold,
Torchlight crimson on the copper kettle-drums,
Then the tuckets, then the trumpets, then the cannon,
and he comes.
Don John laughing in the brave beard curled,
Spurning of his stirrups like the thrones of all the world,
Holding his head up for a flag of all the free.

G. K. CHESTERTON, *Lepanto*

(*bb*) I saw within the wheelwright's shed
The big round cartwheels, blue and red;
A plough with blunted share;
A blue tin jug; a broken chair;
And paint in trial patchwork square
Slapped up against the wall;
The lumber of the wheelwright's trade,
And tools on benches neatly laid,
The brace, the adze, the awl.

V. SACKVILLE-WEST, *Making Cider*

(cc)
Ah, here it is! the sliding rail
  That marks the old remembered spot,—
The gap that struck our schoolboy trail,—
  The crooked path across the lot.

It left the road by school and church,
  A pencilled shadow, nothing more,
That parted from the silver birch
  And ended at the farm-house door.

O. W. HOLMES, *The Crooked Footpath*

(dd)
How beautiful is night!
  A dewy freshness fills the silent air;
No mist obscures, nor cloud, nor speck, nor stain,
    Breaks the serene of heaven;
  In full-orbed glory yonder moon divine
    Rolls through the dark blue depths.
      Beneath her steady ray
      The desert-circle spreads,
  Like the round ocean, girdled with the sky.
    How beautiful is night!

R. SOUTHEY, *Thalaba*

(ee)
See on the mountain's southern side,
Where the prospect opens wide,
Where the ev'ning gilds the tide,
How close and small the hedges lie!
What streaks of meadows cross the eye!
A step, methinks, may pass the stream,
So little distant dangers seem;
So we mistake the future's face,
Ey'd thro' Hope's deluding glass;
As yon' summits soft and fair,
Clad in colours of the air,
Which, to those who journey near,
Barren, brown, and rough appear;
Still we tread the same coarse way;
The present's still a cloudy day.

JOHN DYER, *Grongar Hill*

(ff)   A casement high and triple-arch'd there was,
       All garlanded with carven imageries,
       Of fruits and flowers, and bunches of knot-grass,
       And diamonded with panes of quaint device,
       Innumerable of stains and splendid dyes,
       As are the tiger-moth's deep-damask'd wings;
       And in the midst, 'mong thousand heraldries,
       And twilight saints, and dim emblazonings,
   A shielded scutcheon blush'd with blood of queens and kings.

J. KEATS, *The Eve of St Agnes*

For EU product safety concerns, contact us at Calle de José Abascal, 56–1°,
28003 Madrid, Spain or eugpsr@cambridge.org.

www.ingramcontent.com/pod-product-compliance
Ingram Content Group UK Ltd.
Pitfield, Milton Keynes, MK11 3LW, UK
UKHW012327130625
459647UK00009B/124